LANCASTRIANS, YORKISTS, AND HENRY VII

Henry VII

Bust by Pietro Torregiano, Victoria & Albert Museum

LANCASTRIANS
YORKISTS
AND HENRY VII

BY

S. B. CHRIMES
Professor of History, University College, Cardiff

LONDON
MACMILLAN & CO LTD
NEW YORK · ST MARTIN'S PRESS
1964

MACMILLAN AND COMPANY LIMITED
St Martin's Street London WC 2
also Bombay Calcutta Madras Melbourne

THE MACMILLAN COMPANY OF CANADA LIMITED
Toronto

ST MARTIN'S PRESS INC
New York

PRINTED IN GREAT BRITAIN

For My Wife

Contents

List of Illustrations

*The cover design shows the Arms of England
1198–1340, 1340–1405 and 1405–1603*

Preface

No period in English history has been the subject of such powerful literary presentation as the fifteenth century. Shakespeare's perception of the dramatic quality of the main political and dynastic events which made up the central theme in the history of England from the accession of Richard II to the death of Richard III, and the extraordinary skill with which he used the material then available to sustain the story through eight plays, have given to the century an unique renown.

The high dramatic value of these plays, and the general fidelity with which he followed the historical material accessible to him, are not in doubt. But the Tudor chroniclers' conceptions of the events of the fifteenth century, immortalized as they have become through these plays, are not the same as those of modern historians. Those chronicles are not read much nowadays except by scholars, but Shakespeare's history plays continue to be read, acted, filmed, or broadcast, and their version of history has been brought home to millions. It is, however, not easy for the general reading public to obtain a straightforward account of what really happened in the course of what is commonly called the period of the 'Wars of the Roses'. There are still indeed a great many things in that period about which we do not know as much as we should like. The fifteenth century is even yet the 'Cinderella' period of English history, and much research on modern lines needs to be done before we can hope to know all that we might about it.

The present writer, however, has thought it worth while to recount in comparatively brief space the course of events which dominated the dynastic history of the period, dictated the circumstances of the 'Wars of the Roses' which provided the background, and in a large degree the foundations, for the work of the first Tudor sovereign. One hopes that this small book's readers will thereby be brought to a better understanding of a fascinating even if puzzling period in our history, and at the same time to a better appreciation of the realities behind the dramatic version which more than three hundred years ago was unfolded once and for all.

It deserves to be made quite clear at the start that there is no historical justification for the term 'Wars of the Roses'. We need to grasp firmly that no contemporary ever thought of the civil wars of the period in such terms, nor indeed ever used the expression at all. The first person to use it appears to have been that great historical romancer, Sir Walter Scott, in 1829 (*Anne of Geierstein*, ch. vii). True, many of the Tudor chroniclers and propagandists made literary play with the two Roses, and expatiated about their 'union' by the marriage of Henry Tudor and Elizabeth of York, and so forth, but they stopped short of calling the series of battles 'the wars of the roses'. The men who fought those battles from 1455 onwards certainly knew nothing of such flights of literary fancy. We can be quite sure that the rose-plucking scene in the Temple garden so vividly depicted by Shakespeare in 1 *Henry VI*, II. iv, never took place in reality. But it will indeed be a long time before we outlive so splendid an invention of the dramatist's imagination.

The fact is that there is no evidence of the use of the red rose as a badge by Henry VI at all. The heraldic badges used by the noble families of the period were numerous and varied. The same person might use different badges at different times and places, or at the same time, according as he was for the moment being regarded as the duke of this, or the earl of that, or the lord of such and such domain, or as the king. One and the same man might of course be all these things at once. For their descents were variegated and complex, and badges were inherited or acquired by marriage along with the landed estates whose tenants or retainers actually wore the appropriate badge. Thus Edmund, earl of Lancaster, in the fourteenth century used a red rose as badge, whereas Henry, first duke of Lancaster used not only the red rose, but also three or four other badges, some of which he naturally employed before he became Lancaster. John of Gaunt in his turn did much the same, and made use of at least five other badges. His son, Henry IV, utilized no fewer than fourteen badges at one time or another, of which the red rose was by no means the most prominent. Henry V also used a number, including the red rose, but Henry VI apparently resorted to only four, of which the red rose was not one. Richard, duke of York, did use a white rose among other badges, but only because he inherited it from his Mortimer ancestors. His son, Edward IV, continued to use it, but only among ten others of various derivations. Richard III had his own personal badge of the white boar long before he became king, and there is no evidence that he usurped the white rose (though he did get a rose on to his Great Seal); for if the white rose belonged to anyone, it was to the descendants of Edward IV, and by them it was used. Richard III, however, could take over for some purposes Edward IV's favourite badge, which he had invented for himself after Mortimer's Cross — the sun in splendour.

It remained open to Henry VII to revive the red rose to emphasize such Lancastrian pretensions as he had, and eventually to invent the Tudor Rose for himself and his heirs by superimposing a white upon a red rose; but he used also the portcullis which he derived from his Beaufort ancestors, and sundry other badges, including, naturally in the circumstances, and for some purposes, the red dragon of Cadwallader.

'The Wars of the Roses', therefore, existed, and could exist, only as a figment of retrospective imagination. The dynastic civil wars to which the misleading label came to be applied were not in fact fought between the supporters of rival symbols; they did not kill or were killed for the sake of rival roseate badges. They contended for the realities of political power. For that reason the present writer has avoided using the term at all, even though he can scarcely hope that others will readily follow his example in this perhaps, by now, pedantic renunciation.[1]

S.B.C.

University College

Cardiff

[1] It should be noted, however, that Professor E. F. Jacob has published his *The Fifteenth Century* in the Oxford History of England (1961) without once using the term in his text.

Acknowledgments

The publishers are indebted to the following to reproduce the illustrations on the pages quoted:

British Museum, pp. 2, 11, 19, 22, 25, 26, 35, 36, 44, 47, 49, 54, 56, 62, 64, 66, 129, 151.

His Grace the Lord Archbishop of Canterbury and the Trustees of Lambeth Palace Library, p. 112.

The Lord Chamberlain (by gracious permission of Her Majesty The Queen), pp. 93, 106, 144.

The Clerk of the Council and Keeper of the Records of the Duchy of Lancaster (Photograph supplied by the Controller of H.M. Stationary Office. Crown copyright), p. 43.

G. B. Mason, Esq., p. 71.

Victoria and Albert Museum (Crown copyright), frontispiece and p. 63.

The Dean and Chapter of Westminster, pp. 31, 51, 155, 157, 173. (Photographs on pp. 31, 155, 157 supplied by the Warburg Institute)

Ministry of Works (Crown copyright), p. 59.

The Syndics of the Cambridge University Press, for the map at the end of the volume from *The Cambridge Medieval History*.

The author is indebted to David Piper Esq., of the National Portrait Gallery, for helpful advice on the portraits.

The Genesis of Lancaster and York

WHEN, at the age of sixty-five, Edward III's life came to an end on 21 June, 1377, he had reigned for fifty years. Only one king of England before him (Henry III), and one king (George III) and one queen (Victoria) after him, have so far reigned for a longer period. During that half-century, the course of events, for very many years conditioned by the king's own policies and activities, had materially changed the character and fortunes of the realm. England had become England in a sense in which she had never been in the past. She had become nationally self-conscious to a degree unprecedented. She had avenged the humiliation of Bannockburn by a judicious use of the long-bow (the efficacy of which in the hands of the Welsh hillsmen had been discerned by Edward's grandfather and which in improved form was now to become the all-powerful English weapon), at the battle of Halidon Hill (1331). She had rounded-off that triumph by the capture of King David II at Neville's Cross in 1346 and by compelling his involuntary residence in the Tower of London for eleven years. The Scottish problem (as the English saw it) had thus been settled for a generation. England had also for the first time stepped into the front rank of European military powers in consequence of Edward III's great victory over the French and overwhelming odds at Crécy in 1346, his capture of Calais in 1347, and of his son the Black Prince's repetition of his father's feat, at Poitiers, in 1356. The pride and prestige flowing to her from the fact that the king of France was

B

*Edward III invests Edward, prince of Wales
(The Black Prince) with the duchy of Acquitaine, 1362*

(*De Pace Franciae et Angliae,* B.M. Cottonian MS. Nero D VI,
fo. 31)

obliged to take up his lodgings in the same London residence which David II, king of Scots, had by then just left, and to stay there for four years pending agreement on his ransom and terms for a treaty of peace, were unbounded. The ransom-monies for less exalted captives and plunder in the wars had brought affluence to many an English (and Welsh) warrior, according to his degree. Family fortunes reaped the profits of the Hundred Years' War — for a time.

The realm had suffered the ravages of the Black Death, and recovered, albeit with a substantially diminished population. But the glories of the reign had not by any means been confined to feats of arms and endurance. It had also been the age of Chaucer, and had seen the first fine flowering of English vernacular literature; latterly it had also become the age of Wycliffe and religious ferment. The slow but sure amalgam of Norman and Anglo-Saxon had come to fruition.

The England of 1377 was something quite different from the England of 1327. Not only had its international position changed out of recognition; not only had its achievements in many spheres enhanced its sense of national cohesion and character; the very nature of its government had altered. The parliament of England, although by no means new, having existed in some form or another for a hundred years or so, was not the same thing in 1377 as it had been in 1327. There could indeed still be 'parliaments' or great councils of magnates without the Commons, but the king had found himself unable to finance his French campaigns, fought as they had been on a larger scale and for longer periods than ever before, without frequent recourse to the money grants of the Commons in parliaments. The Hundred Years' War had determined that the administrative centre, the capital, should be Westminster; it went far also to determine that parliaments with the Commons, should be frequent, almost

annual, and that the monarchy should become regularly
dependent upon the Commons in parliaments for financial
aid. In theory, the king was to continue for a long time 'to
live of his own', i.e. to rely upon his own hereditary
revenues, perquisites, and large, expensive borrowings, to
defray the ordinary expenses of his government; but in
practice these expenses seldom remained 'ordinary'.
'Extraordinary' expenses could only be met with the aid of
parliamentary grants of taxation. The king's financial
needs, therefore, made the presence of the Commons in
parliament a frequent necessity, and their summons a
governmental habit. But he who pays the piper can always
call part at least of the tune, and by the time of the 'Good'
parliament of 1376, it had become possible for the Commons to organize and launch a far-reaching attack on the
conduct and policies of the government, and yet still be
allowed to remain in session for more than two months.
Much of their work could be undone, it is true, by the
exercise of suitable influence in the next parliament, but
the day had gone by when the Commons in parliament
could be reckoned with and merely discounted.

Furthermore, the last years of the reign had seen a
marked decline in the personal exercise of the powers of
the monarchy by the king himself. Edward III lived to be
an old man by contemporary standards, and outlived his
energies and faculties. His vitality had become sapped by
the strains and stresses, and eventual disappointment of
his life's work — the French war. The great victories of
Crécy and Poitiers, the capture of King John of France,
and the Treaty of Brétigny of 1360, in spite of all their
superficial brilliance, brought success the hollowness of
which could not in the long run be concealed. The Treaty
had purported to restore to the Crown of England
substantially all the territorial possessions of the Angevin
kings south of the Loire, but by 1375 the Treaty of Bruges
perforce ended the fighting for Edward III's reign, and

left him with little but Calais, Bordeaux, Bayonne, and Ponthieu. Disillusionment brought bitterness to Edward III's personal decline; disappointment and enfeeblement combined to impair his effectiveness as head of the government, and promoted the passage of power to a Council acting in his name but dominated by others than himself. It was a situation which inevitably encouraged the ambitions of his numerous sons, but not for very long in the case of his natural successor, his first-born son. For Edward the Black Prince died a year before his father.

Edward III, in addition to his other achievements, holds the record among English kings for the number of his children by one wife; for the number of his sons; and above all for the number of his sons who survived to have lawful issue of their own, and so to bedevil the politics and complicate the family connexions of the peerage for the next hundred years and more. Edward III had barely passed his fifteenth year when he married his second cousin, Philippa, daughter of William the Good, count of Hainault, one year after his accession, four months after his father Edward II had been done to death in Berkeley Castle at the instigation of his wife Isabella and her paramour Roger Mortimer, earl of March, under whose joint régime Edward III subsisted until 1330. For twenty-five years, from 1330 to 1355, Philippa dutifully presented her husband with a sucession of twelve children: seven sons and five daughters. Of these seven sons, only two died young and without issue. Of the daughters, three died young and without issue; whilst the other two made marriages and had issue not of major importance in the course of events. It was from among the five surviving sons that the future dynastic difficulties were to come. They and their descendants, or some of them, were to develop ambitions and rivalries which were destined to determine the course of political events in England for a hundred and fifty years after the nuptials of Edward III and Philippa. In the long run, descent from Edward III was to be more than dangerous; it was to become practically equivalent to a sentence of death (unless you happened to descend by one particular strand), as no doubt Margaret, countess of Salisbury, reflected when in 1541 Henry VIII had the head off her shoulders because of her descent and its temptations.

But Edward III naturally could not foresee the future when in 1337, following the custom of France, whose king he was soon to claim to be, he set a precedent in England by creating a dukedom for his first-born son, Edward, who six years later was also to become the second (English) prince of Wales. Having thus started this exaltation of his male offspring by making Edward duke of Cornwall, doubtless he could not stop at that point. His second son died before any ducal provision could be made for him; but his third son, Lionel (of Antwerp) became duke of Clarence in 1362, on the same day as his fourth son John (of Ghent, *anglicé* Gaunt) became duke of Lancaster. The long interval between the first and the second of these creations suggests that perhaps Edward III harboured doubts about the desirability of multiplying the number of royal dukes. At any rate he did not see fit to create any more of them himself. It was left to his fifth son, Edmund (of Langley) and his seventh son, Thomas (of Woodstock) — the sixth died in infancy — to procure from their as yet (in 1385) still pliable nephew Richard II, the dukedoms of York and of Gloucester respectively.

The first five royal dukes had thus come into existence, but of these, as it turned out, there were never to be more than three in being at any one time, and by 1399, only two survived — Lancaster and York. The first duke of Cornwall, Edward, prince of Wales, died in 1376, leaving his second and only surviving son Richard to succeed to the throne on 22 June, 1377, at the age of ten. Richard II was destined to die leaving no issue. The first duke of Clarence,

Lionel, died in 1368, leaving only a daughter, Philippa — of whom more later.[1] The first duke of Gloucester, Thomas, was put to death at Calais in 1397 at the instigation of his royal nephew Richard II — by then less pliant and more embittered. The first (royal) duke of Lancaster, John, survived until 3 February, 1399, when he was fifty-eight, and the first duke of York, Edmund, until 1 August, 1402, when he was sixty-one. It was the progeny of these two, John and Edmund, together with that of their elder brother Lionel, which between them were to give rise to the famous 'Houses' of Lancaster and of York, and so to determine much of the high politics of fifteenth-century England.

John of Gaunt was married three times, but fortunately was not responsible for more than two male lines of descent. At the tender age of two and half years, he had been made earl of Richmond, and at nineteen he had married the lady who was to bring him Lancaster and to provide him with his first-born son — Blanche, daughter and heiress of his father's most distinguished and favoured counsellor and companion-in-arms, Henry of Grosmont, earl of Derby and of Lincoln by creation, of Lancaster by inheritance from his own father (a grandson of Henry III), and first duke of Lancaster by creation in 1351. John of Gaunt in 1361 succeeded in the right of his wife to the vast territorial possessions of the duchy, and was granted the dukedom itself in 1362. Four years later, Blanche, after having had two daughters (one of whom became queen of Portugal), gave birth at Bolingbroke to a son — Henry, who was destined in time to become king of England as Henry IV. But Blanche died in 1369 (as did also Queen Philippa), and John of Gaunt, by then the greatest magnate in the realm, in 1371 married Constance, the heiress of Castile. By virtue of this alliance he claimed, without much more than titular success, to be king of Castile and Leon. By her he

[1] See p. 13 below.

had only a daughter, who eventually consoled her father's monarchial disappointment by marrying the real king of Castile, and thereby passed out of English history.

But in the meantime, John of Gaunt had found in less distinguished quarters an *inamorata*, whom many years later he was to make his third duchess, and, as it turned out, the ancestress of all the sovereigns of England subsequent to Henry VI and of all the sovereigns of Scotland subsequent to James I. He himself, naturally, in the process became lineal ancestor of all those English and Scottish sovereigns (as well as of the sovereigns of Portugal and Castile-Aragon through his daughters by his first two wives); but he could scarcely have foreseen such contingencies when his mistress Katherine Swynford in or about 1373 gave birth to the first of three bastard sons, not to mention a daughter, of his begetting. John, Henry, and Thomas Beaufort (as they were called after a castle in Champagne which had formerly belonged to Lancaster) had been begot, and as half-brothers to Henry of Bolingbroke they and their descendants were to complicate the political and family scene until in the fulness of time one of their line was to occupy the throne itself. If indeed these Beaufort brothers had remained bastards, little would have been heard of them, but legally they did not so remain. There could not, indeed, be any question of legitimation for them for many years after their birth. When John of Gaunt first cast amorous eyes upon Katherine Swynford, he was a lawfully married man, and for that matter Katherine was most probably a lawfully wedded wife. Her father, Sir Payne Roelt, had come to England in the train of Philippa of Hainault, and Katherine had become a lady in attendance upon John's first wife Blanche. A husband had been found for her from among his household, and she had become the wife of Sir Hugh Swynford (a squire of Anglo-Saxon descent and small means), and by him she became the mother of one Sir Thomas Swynford. Sir Hugh passed away in 1372. An exact date cannot be put upon the beginning of the liaison of John and Katherine, nor upon the birth of their eldest son John Beaufort, but certainly this latter event took place early enough to suggest that the loving couple were not excessively strict in observing the chronological proprieties. Since unquestionably all three Beaufort boys were born during the life-time of John of Gaunt's second wife, who did not die until 1394, all three reached manhood before any possible prospect of legitimation could arise. Nor could any such prospect materialize unless John of Gaunt were prepared first to make his faithful mistress of twenty-five years' standing not only a respectable woman, but also a royal duchess of the highest estate. The remarkable thing was that he was so prepared, and did do so. What satisfaction this consummation may have given to the couple, we know not, but the decision was momentous. It was to give the future Henry Tudor a line of descent from Edward III.

It could not have been at all an easy decision to take nor to implement. It was no light matter for the duke of Lancaster (and of Acquitaine) and titular king of Castile, the senior surviving son of Edward III and the senior uncle of the reigning king, to make a woman of Katherine's modest status and antecedents into his lawful duchess. But as it happened, Richard II at the time had strong reasons for being anxious to please his uncle, and he not only sanctioned the wedding but also agreed to recognize the new duchess. John and Katherine accordingly became man and wife in July, 1396. Legitimation of bastards by the subsequent matrimony of the parents was a doctrine agreeable to the canon law of the Church, but not to the law of England until 1926, and if the Beaufort boys were to have the benefit of their parents' nuptials, further arrangements were needed. The Church made no difficulties in the circumstances, and Pope Boniface IX obliged by pronouncing the boys legitimate on 1 September,

1396, whilst Richard II set them right in the law of England by granting letters patent of legitimation which for good measure were confirmed in the parliament of 1397. The children's half-brother Henry Bolingbroke might, later on as Henry IV, make more than mental reservations about the scope of this act, but the deed was done. There was no impediment now to John Beaufort's becoming earl and marquis of Somerset, nor to Henry Beaufort's becoming bishop and cardinal in due course, nor to Thomas Beaufort's becoming in time duke of Exeter. Nor indeed any reason why any of them or their descendants should not become keen and energetic promoters of, and participants in, the fortunes of the House of Lancaster. Nor any reason why their sister, Joan Beaufort, should not in due course become the second wife to her second husband, Ralph Neville, first earl of Westmorland, and add to his quiverful of seven children by his first wife a further nine offspring, the youngest of whom was to be Cicely, the future wife of Richard, duke of York, and mother of Kings Edward IV and Richard III.

In the meantime, John of Gaunt's next younger brother, Edmund of Langley, a man of lesser personality and virility, had been having his matrimonial experiences, and was inaugurating the history, albeit a far more chequered history than he knew, of the House of York. Edmund, born in 1341, had been made earl of Cambridge in 1362, and had married in 1371 Isabel, second daughter of Pedro the Cruel of Castile and the sister of his brother John's second wife Constance, shortly after the latter two were married. The Spanish strain from Constance went back to Spain with her daughter Katherine's marriage to the eventual Henry III, king of Castile, but the same strain from Isabel remained at home to colour, no doubt, the temperaments of the future Yorkists. Isabel, however, died in 1392, and Edmund then married Joan, daughter of Thomas Holland II, earl of Kent, but had no issue by her. He had already

*John Beaufort, earl and marquis of Somerset
(d. 1410) and his wife Margaret Holland.
Before 1399*

(B.M. Royal MS. 2 A XVIII, fo. 23b)

had by Isabel two sons and a daughter. Both these sons were dead before the end of 1415, but for very different reasons. The elder of them, Edward, created earl of Rutland by his cousin, Richard II, in 1390, and duke of Albemarle in 1397, but deprived in 1399 of the latter title by his other cousin, Henry IV, succeeded his father (who had been created duke of York in 1385) in 1402. He loyally supported his cousins of Lancaster, only, however, to lose his life at Agincourt on 25 October, 1415; and, although he was already married, he died without issue. Edmund's second son, Richard, had been promoted to be earl of Cambridge by Henry V in 1414, but impatient of his cousin of Lancaster's royal estate, and for reasons of his own which will appear shortly, he lent himself to overt treason against Henry V on the eve of the expedition which was destined to lead to Agincourt, and lost his head, precipitately but legally, in the August of the year in which his elder brother was to die a less ignominious death.

By the end of October, 1415, with the second duke killed and his brother executed and attainted, the prospects for the House of York were very dim; they would have been slight indeed, and dependent by then only upon a junior female line represented by the progeny of the younger daughter of Edward's and Richard's sister — if it had not been for the all-important fact that Richard did not suffer execution before he too had married (twice) and begotten a son (by his first wife), named Richard after him. This boy Richard was allowed in due course to succeed to his deceased uncle's dukedom of York. Maybe Henry of Lancaster would have found more difficulty in permitting this to happen if he had known that this Richard was to become *the* duke of York who in the fulness of time was destined to contest with Lancaster the very throne itself, and whose son Edward was to oust the heir of Lancaster, Henry VI, altogether.

But when that time came, it was less Richard of York's paternal than his maternal descent that enabled him to make a plausible claim to be the rightful heir of Edward III. It was his mother rather than his father who mattered most in that connexion. For his mother was Ann Mortimer, grand-daughter of him who had once been the second surviving son of Edward III, namely, Lionel, duke of Clarence.

The name of Mortimer has so far been mentioned only once in this Prologue, in respect of that Roger Mortimer, earl of March, whose liaison with Edward III's mother Isabella, had resulted in the deposition and murder of Edward II, and who had in due time been eliminated by Edward III and his friends. The Mortimers of Wigmore were a tough and turbulent family firmly and powerfully entrenched in the Welsh Marches, and it was a matter of great consequence that Roger Mortimer's great-grandson Edmund should have been allowed to marry so important an heiress as Philippa — Lionel, duke of Clarence's only child. For their son, Roger III, earl of March, inevitably became, in the absence of any heir apparent, Richard II's heir presumptive, until 20 July, 1398, when he died, killed in trying to cope, as the king's lieutenant, with an Irish uprising. This event was to serve as the pretext for Richard II's second and last fateful expedition to Ireland in the following year. Roger III left behind him as the next heir presumptive his son Edmund, a boy then of only six years of age: the lawful heir of Richard II, but far too young and friendless to be able to assert himself when in that year Henry of Bolingbroke decided to put himself forward as the claimant.

But Edmund Mortimer was not without the advantage of having marriageable sisters, and it had been none other than the eldest of these (and his eventual sole heiress), Ann, whom Richard, earl of Cambridge, had married, and it was largely, if not entirely, on behalf of the slighted claims of his brother-in-law Edmund, that Richard had participated in the premature plot which brought him to the block in 1415. The more discreet Edmund lived on, unharmed, until 1425, but though married, died without issue, thus leaving a clear field for his sister Ann's son, Richard, duke of York, to make what he could of the fact that he was descended (even if through two females) from Edward III's second surviving son, and also (through males only) from his fourth surviving son, whilst the descendant of the third surviving son, Henry VI, held the sceptre by virtue of his grandfather's ousting of Richard II.

Thus it was that the fates played unkind tricks with the progeny of the victor of Crécy. Well might that doughty warrior have turned in his grave if he had known the temptations, provocations, and tribulations that destiny had in store for his children's children. For more, much more, than a hundred years after he had been gathered to his fathers, no one could say with certainty in which of the several streams emanating from him the sovereignty would ultimately lie. Yet in the long run he could have comforted himself with the thought that that sovereignty would never altogether pass away from one or other of those streams, thin, very thin, though that persistent stream might become. In spite of all, the blood of Edward III and of all his forbears from William the Conqueror still flows, even though through channels undreamt of by him or by any of them.

The Rise and Fall of Lancaster

To appreciate the circumstances and meaning of the rise of the House of Lancaster, it is necessary to look back a little beyond the life-time of John of Gaunt, for the vast accumulation of estates which came to him by his highly remunerative marriage with Blanche of Lancaster did not originate with him or her. The foundations of the great apanage were laid in the time of John of Gaunt's great-great-grandfather, Henry III, for the benefit of the younger of his two surviving sons, Edmund Crouchback, and built largely out of the territorial windfalls of rebellion. The death of the famous Simon de Montfort, earl of Leicester, at the battle of Evesham in 1265, and the death or punishment of other rebels about that time, brought to the king a fine haul of forfeited estates. The extensive lands of Simon de Montfort, spread over twelve counties, together with the earldom and honour of Leicester, were promptly granted to Edmund, and these were followed by those of Robert Ferrars, earl of Derby. The latter transference could only be accomplished by a good deal of unscrupulous chicanery; for Robert Ferrars had rebelled after the battle of Evesham, was not dead at the time, and according to the terms of the ultimate pacification he was entitled to redeem his lands at a price. The terms for him, however, were put impossibly high, and his lands stayed in Edmund's tenacious grip. But neither Edmund nor his son Thomas claimed to be earl of Derby.

A very substantial nucleus of territory had thus come into the hands of Henry III's favoured son, but still more

was to come. On 30 June, 1267, Edmund was created earl
of Lancaster, and granted the honour, county, town, and
castle of Lancaster, all the royal demesne lands in the
county, the waste lands and forests of Wynesdale and
Lonsdale, the town of Newcastle-under-Lyme, and the
honour and castle of Pickering in Yorkshire. By a royal
charter all these lands were to be held quit of suit of shire
and hundred courts and of sheriff's aids, and free from
many other customary dues. The main foundations of the
inheritance of Lancaster had in this way been firmly laid
by 1268, and there were to be no major additions to it by
royal grant for a century.

Edmund had come into a very handsome property,
located in no fewer than 632 places in England and Wales,
with forty-nine demesne manors in his own hands (i.e.
without tenants holding from him), and with seven castles
of importance (Leicester, Lancaster, Tutbury, Kenilworth,
Grosmont, Skenfrith, and Whitecastle), as well as lesser
ones. His properties, especially prolific in the shires of
Derby, Stafford, Leicester, and Northampton, and in the
Trent valley, where he was by far the greatest lord, were to
be found, piece by piece, spread from the Lancashire to
the Yorkshire coasts, and from South Wales to the Scots
Border. He could scarcely complain, therefore, that his
father had not done very well by him. But Edmund's
acquisitive instincts soon found other outlets. He was
granted the right to marry Isabel de Redvers, widow of
William de Fors, earl of Aumale and Holderness, but
preferred the hand of her daughter Eveline, then ten years
of age, and consoled himself for her tender age (and her
death five years later) with the comforting thought that
she was the sole heiress of the Aumale inheritance, and
through her mother, of the earldom of Devon and the
lordship of the Isle of Wight. Freed from his short-lived
but not unprofitable matrimonial adventure, he cast his
eyes further afield and espied a desirable widow in Blanche

of Artois, widow of Henry, king of Navarre and count of Champagne. Very inconveniently Navarre had recently been overrun by the French and was not to be acquired by merely a matrimonial alliance; but Champagne came with Blanche, and Edmund could for some years properly call himself count of Champagne. Included in the Champagne acquisition was the lordship and castle of Beaufort, which, however, was destined to be irremediably lost to the king of France in 1369, but which, as we have noted, was to come in useful later still as a surname for John of Gaunt's nameless brood.

Edmund ended his terrestrial acquisitions on 5 June, 1296, and the greater part passed to his son Thomas, second earl of Lancaster, then a minor, but who was deemed to be of age in 1298, and who did homage and was duly put into possession. Thomas's career was to prove very nearly fatal to the integrity of the inheritance of Lancaster, for he was destined to lose it all and his head with it, at the hands of his cousin Edward II, as the due reward for his truculent turbulence and overt treason. Thomas did not at any time receive much additional endowment by royal grant, but nevertheless was able by his marriage to the wealthy Alice Lucy, heiress of the earls of Salisbury and Lincoln, to add materially to his estates, and to the number of his earldoms and of his major castles. Included among those were Pontefract in Yorkshire and Bolingbroke in Lincolnshire, both of which were to acquire later a notoriety unforeseeable by him. These territories remained with him to the end, but his wife Alice found that she had had enough of him after a few years of matrimony, and under the protection of John Warrene, earl of Surrey, deserted him, finding consolation elsewhere.

Politics, or what passed for politics, in the reign of Edward II proved to be Thomas's undoing. His opposition to the king, and his high-handed even if rather low-witted

c

tactics were successful for some years, and brought to him great prominence and influence. He became the leader among the Lords Ordainers who sought to constrain the king in the exercise of his prerogatives in 1310–11. He was privy to the murder of Edward II's favourite *protégé*, Peter Gaveston, in 1312; he failed to support the king at Bannockburn in 1314 and so helped to lose that battle for England; he even entered into treasonable correspondence with the Scots under the ludicrous pseudonym of 'King Arthur'. But any kingship he may have aspired to remained mythical. His five earldoms were not enough to save him in the long run from the consequences of his misdeeds. His fate was to be proclaimed rebel in February, 1322, to be defeated at Boroughbridge, to be tried for treason in his own castle of Pontefract in the presence of the king, condemned, and beheaded on 22 March. All his estates were declared forfeit.

The House of Lancaster might indeed have fallen finally there and then, had not Thomas left behind him, not a son, but a brother, Henry, who had not been involved in his brother's schemes, and who well knew how to wring the changes out of the wheel of fortune. His petitionings for restoration did not go altogether unheeded even by Edward II; he got back from him the county, honour, and the title of earl, of Leicester, as well as sundry other minor properties. But to get back Lancaster he had recourse to other methods. He sided with Isabella and Mortimer in their *coup d'état* against Edward II, and they were not slow to reward him with the partial restoration of Lancaster when he succeeded in capturing the person of Edward II and in holding him prisoner in the Lancastrian castle of Kenilworth towards the end of 1326. A full restitution to him followed of all the lands which had been held by Thomas on the day he died. Henry was clearly a skilful trimmer, and contrived — almost prematurely for his own safety — to defect from Isabella and Mortimer soon

Henry, duke of Lancaster, sets sail to Calais

(*Chroniques de France ou de St. Denis*, B.M. Royal MS. 20,
C VII, fo. 184b)

enough to procure from Edward III a confirmation of all
his restitutions.

Further and great advancement was left to his son and
heir Henry of Grosmont, created earl of Derby by Edward
III in 1337. Henry of Grosmont redeemed his family's
somewhat dubious repute by loyally serving Edward III
as soldier and counsellor in the French wars, in the course
of which he acquired not only the lordship of Bergerac, but
a European prestige for his martial and chivalrous conduct,
so that no incongruity was felt when in 1351 Edward set
another precedent by creating him the first duke of
Lancaster and elevating the dignity of Lancaster into a
county palatine. The great duchy of Lancaster had thus

come into being, and has never ceased to exist to this day.

Henry was indeed greatly favoured, for no county palatine had been created for very many years, and only two others were in existence at the time — Chester and Durham — and no more were ever to be created. The privileges conveyed were great. The grant meant, in brief, that the duke, in his county palatine, could exercise most of the powers of the king himself. Not the king's writ, but the duke's writ, issuable from his own chancery and under the great seal of the duchy, ran. The duke, not the king, appointed the justices for hearing pleas of the crown, and executed the judgments by his own writs and officers, and appointed the sheriff of the shire. The duke himself could nominate two knights of the shire and two burgesses of each borough to sit in parliaments. He could do many other things profitable and useful, though he could not do everything. The king reserved to himself his normal royal financial rights (even if the duke appointed the collectors thereof), as well as the power to pardon and to correct errors in jurisdiction.

For ten years Henry was spared to enjoy his dukedom and his extraordinary privileges, but then he in his turn placed the integrity of the duchy in jeopardy by leaving only two daughters, his co-heiresses, Maude and Blanche. Maude had by then married as her second husband William of Hainault, duke of Zeeland, and had passed out of English affairs. But Blanche was obviously a promising match for the king's third surviving son, John of Gaunt, then earl of Richmond, to whom she was married in 1359. When Henry died in 1362, it looked as though, in accordance with law the inheritance would have to be divided up between the co-heiresses, and steps in that direction were actually taken. But Maude very obligingly also passed away, childless, in 1362, and thus made Blanche an even more admirable spouse for John of Gaunt. For now the whole inheritance came to him, and the dukedom could be given him, and the palatine powers, which had lapsed on the death of the first duke, could be revived for his life (as from 1371). True, the honour of Richmond, which John had previously been given, had to be surrendered to someone else for politic reasons, but ample compensation in lands elsewhere was provided; he was able also to acquire the castle, town, and honour of Hertford, and generally to consolidate his holdings in the midlands. He was to lose, by arson during the Peasants' Revolt in 1381, the great palace of the Savoy in London which Duke Henry had built, and to suffer other damage to some of his properties at that time. The grant to him of the title of duke of Acquitaine in 1390 and his acquisition of interests in Castile by his second marriage brought him no permanent territorial gains. But when the time came he seemed to be in a position to pass on to his son by Blanche a very satisfactory inheritance, improved and rounded off by Richard II's grant to him of the palatine powers to himself and the heirs male of his body, and a charter setting forth the privileges of the duchy. The date of this charter was 29 June, 1396. Within three years, the position was utterly changed, and Lancaster, it seemed, was totally ruined. By then John of Gaunt was dead; his son Henry of Bolingbroke had been banished for life; the whole inheritance of Lancaster was confiscated to the Crown. To understand (so far as it can be understood) how this sharp reversal of fortune came about, we must turn to the career of Henry Bolingbroke during his father's life-time.

Henry had been born on 30 April, 1367, at the castle of Bolingbroke, near Spilsbury in Lincolnshire. He was just old enough to be allowed to bear one of the ceremonial swords at the coronation in 1377 of his cousin Richard II, who was seven months younger than himself.

In the same year one of his father's numerous inherited

John of Gaunt, duke of Lancaster,
receives a letter from the King of Portugal

(Jean de Waurin, *Chronique d'Angleterre*, B.M. Royal MS.
14 E IV, fo. 236)

titles was passed to him, and he was henceforth for many
years known as the earl of Derby, and some territorial
provision was also made for him — the heir of the greatest
single inheritance in the realm except for one — that of
Richard II himself. Naturally it was desirable that his
more immediate prospects should be improved as soon as
possible, and fortunately a suitable heiress was available

in Mary Bohun, younger daughter of the earl of Hereford. It was awkward that Henry's unscrupulous and assertive youngest uncle, Thomas of Woodstock, then earl of Buckingham, had already perceived the advantages of eventually acquiring as much as he could get of the Hereford inheritance, and had snapped up Mary's elder sister Eleanor, and was interested in the possibility of transforming his wife from a mere co-heiress into a sole heiress by trying to persuade her sister Mary to retire to the cloisters. But the young Henry was not to be frustrated in this way, and put an end to any such schemes by marrying his Mary and half of the Hereford inheritance about 1380. It is not fanciful to suppose that although Henry was to be associated with Thomas of Woodstock in opposing and constraining the king their kinsman, their relations were never to be as close or cordial as they might have been but for this episode.

It would be more fanciful to pretend to trace the process whereby the relations between Henry and Richard became so early poisoned and embittered, and fraught with ultimate tragedy. It is less difficult to see why Thomas of Woodstock, duke of Gloucester as he became in 1385, should have sought to exploit to the full the weaknesses and youthful inexperience of his nephew the king, who indeed was only twelve years younger than Thomas himself, but who had succeeded to the throne which Thomas's eldest brother the Black Prince would have enjoyed if only he had lived a little longer. The 'wicked uncle' theme is common enough in legend and history, at any rate from the time of the next duke of Gloucester (who became Richard III), but it was Thomas who set the precedent and did his best to fulfil the role. His ambition for more power, his unscrupulous exploitation of the situation, and his hypocritical pretensions were not exceptional in the history of wicked uncles; what were more unusual were his extraordinary violence, his brutality, and his zest for the wanton shedding of innocent blood. 'The evil that men do lives after them', and much of the blood-thirstiness of English politics in the late fourteenth and the fifteenth centuries is traceable back to Thomas of Woodstock's lust for the blood of his victims.

Henry of Bolingbroke could not, of course, pretend to the role of wicked uncle in his relations with Richard, but the fates nonetheless had played dangerous tricks with him and his cousin the king. For, of the descendants of Edward III in the second generation, these two young men of almost identical age were as yet the only two who counted. Indeed, the only other males of their generation who were to count for anything much were Henry's own half-brothers — the three Beaufort males, who as yet were only bastards with uncertain and dubious prospects. But by the accidents of life, Richard had already become king, whilst Henry in the normal course could expect little for himself, except by his cousin's grace and favour, until such distant date as his father the duke of Lancaster should make way for him. Fate had already gone far to determine that the relations between the cousins would be either cordial or cold, according to the personal characters and temperaments of the two. They could scarcely for long continue to be without incident. Their similarity in birth combined with their disparity in status was too striking not to provoke friction once it became clear that any personal bonds of friendship between them would not be strong enough to keep the inherent danger latent.

One does not know the thoughts that may have run through the minds of the two boys when together they looked out from the Tower of London upon the perils seething around them during the Peasants' Revolt of 1381, or when at that time Richard was able to distinguish himself above all others by his display of manly courage and kingly decision. No such distinction as yet came Henry's way, nor any particular marks of good will from

Richard II holds court after his coronation, 1377

(Jean de Waurin, *Chronique d'Angleterre*, B.M. Royal MS.
14 E IV, fo. 10. This MS. was executed, probably at Bruges,
late 15th century, for Edward IV.)

his cousin the king. Perhaps it was the apparent lack of
grace from Richard, who was not slow to heap honours,
titles, and grants upon his favoured Robert de Vere, that
drove Henry into association with his uncle Thomas of
Woodstock, with Richard Fitzalan, earl of Arundel,
Thomas Beauchamp, earl of Warwick, and Thomas
Mowbray, earl of Nottingham, in their concerted attack
upon Richard's ministers and friends, and their virtual
seizure of the royal powers by a commission extorted from

*Edmund of Langley, duke of York, Thomas of Woodstock,
duke of Gloucester, and Robert de Vere, duke of Ireland,
dine with Richard II*

(Jean de Waurin, *Chronique d'Angleterre*, B.M. Royal MS.
14 E IV, fo. 265)

Richard in the parliament of 1386. Henry himself indeed
was at that time not even of age and was not summoned to
that parliament, but in the next year he was foremost in
frustrating the military aid which Robert de Vere, earl of
Oxford, duke of Ireland, was bringing up from the Welsh
Marches, by defeating them at Radcot Bridge. What gall
that news must have been to cousin Richard! What deep
thoughts of ultimate revenge on Henry may not have been
planted in his bosom from that day onwards! Planted
indeed, and soon watered by Henry's brash and ill-
mannered jibes at Richard's humiliation when they all got
to London, and nourished further by the subsequent

attainder and flight abroad of the king's beloved Robert de Vere.

Henry, now of age in years if not in wisdom, played a leading role in the Merciless Parliament of 1388, and joined with Gloucester, Arundel, Nottingham, and Warwick, to make the fifth Lord Appellant. He shared with them the responsibility for the series of ruthless, cold-blooded judicial murders by way of the common law procedure of 'appeal' which ensued under a thin cloak of trumped-up legality and pretence of 'principles'. Henry, however, to his credit, risked a quarrel with his uncle of Gloucester by protesting at the inclusion among the victims of the entirely respectable and harmless Sir Simon Burley, whose only sin was that he had been tutor and friend to Richard. It may well be that Henry became sickened by the excesses of his associates, or at least began to question what he had to gain from supporting his uncle the duke against his cousin the king. At any rate he began to veer away from his companions in mercilessness, and moved towards Richard. He was retained on the king's council when Richard was able to declare himself of age and to assume his proper prerogatives in September, 1389, and gradually won, if not perhaps the king's favour, at least the disguising of his hostility. This reduction in tension was doubtless facilitated by Henry's decision to repair abroad and to seek martial exploits and a crusader's repute by fighting with the Teutonic Knights against the 'infidels' in Lithuania and Prussia, in 1390 and 1391. Sobered down by his not wholly gratifying experiences in these adventures, on his return Henry was quiescent for several years, and before long not only did he part company with his former Appellant friends, but actually aided and abetted his cousin when Richard's turn had come. He associated himself with his father John of Gaunt in a violent quarrel with the earl of Arundel in 1393; he was a member of the Council of Regency during Richard's first visit to Ireland; he took a principal part in the negotiations leading to Richard's marriage with Isabel, daughter of Charles VI of France in 1396. He spoke up against his former associates Gloucester, Arundel, and Warwick, when they were arrested on Richard's orders. He joined with his father and his uncle of York in providing troops for Richard's safety during the uncertain months of 1397, when the king was reaching the climax of his 'royalist' *coup d'état*, and he himself made a fierce attack on Arundel in the parliament of September, 1397. What impression was made on his mind when the news came that his uncle Thomas of Woodstock had opportunely 'died' in the recesses of the fortress of Calais, whither Richard had dispatched him, or when Arundel's head fell, or whilst Warwick languished in what consequently became known as the Beauchamp Tower within the Tower, or in prison on the Isle of Man, we do not know. Doubtless more cheerful to him were the tidings that the Commons in parliament had declared that neither he nor Thomas Mowbray, earl of Nottingham, had been moved by malice in making the Appeal in 1388, and that King Richard had thereupon vouchsafed his loyalty and had decided to confer upon him a signal mark of honour by creating him a duke in his father's life-time — duke of Hereford. Henry had escaped Richard's Appeal of the Appellants.

But so had Thomas Mowbray, earl of Nottingham, and he too was now singled out for promotion — to the dukedom of Norfolk. Henry cannot have viewed with any enthusiasm this elevation to ducal honours of a man with no royal blood in his veins; a fourth and 'upstart' duke was one too many, and he showed no reluctance to seize an opportunity for procuring Mowbray's downfall when the chance came, as came it did very soon. Mowbray, it seems, was sufficiently shrewd to feel very uneasy about the turn of events and about Richard II's probable motives and intentions, but was indiscreet enough to confide his doubts to Henry. Richard, he is reported to have said, was not to be trusted even if he swore on God's body. Subsequent events proved him right enough, but what he failed to appreciate was that Henry was not to be trusted cither. Here indeed were the means to encompass Mowbray's ruin. Henry hastened to concert his plans, without stopping to reflect that he might at the same time present Richard with a golden opportunity of ridding himself of both Henry and Mowbray at one stroke. Henry at once went off and 'told his father', John of Gaunt, what had passed between Mowbray and himself, and with all the reckless impetuosity which he had shown previously in his career, proceeded in the parliament of January 1398, to 'appeal' Mowbray of treason. One would have thought that in all the circumstances he would have been shy of appealing the sole remaining Appellant (except himself), who was still both alive and at liberty. His rash and drastic step can only be explained in terms of determination to ruin Mowbray at all costs, and perhaps of a desire to curry favour with Richard. But he miscalculated; he underestimated the slow but steady-burning fires of Richard II's resentment, and perhaps he even failed to appreciate the fairly obvious fact that Richard had by this time achieved for himself untrammelled power as king. The parliament of 1398 was not at all the same kind of arena as that of 1388; the strings were pulled now not by the late unlamented uncle of Gloucester, but by Richard himself, who could readily arrange matters as he wanted them. It cannot have been very difficult to ensure that the matter of the dukes of Hereford and of Norfolk should be an item among the 'unfinished business' of the parliament, and so come on the agenda of the committee of the parliament which had been set up in the ordinary course of procedure, and thus come to be settled outside of the parliament itself. Norfolk had his chance to denounce Hereford as a traitor

in February. The rival accusations could be referred to a
court of chivalry, and a decision be taken that the rivals
should fight it out in the good old feudal style of 'trial by
combat', at Coventry on 16 September. Feeling ran high
in the country at the prospect of such a spectacle. Henry
had retained great popularity as the dashing and vigorous
heir of Lancaster. The crowds descended upon Coventry
as the due date grew near. His very popularity was his
undoing, for Richard could make use of fears of a public
disturbance should the protagonists actually come to
blows, and at the last moment he forbade the duel. With a
further show of concern for the public peace, Richard
could rid the realm (and himself) of both the trouble-
makers by the immediate pronouncement of sentence of
banishment upon both of them — for life in the case of
Mowbray, and with many expressions of regret at the stern
necessity, for ten years (later reduced to six years) in the
case of cousin Henry.

We shall probably never know at just what stage in
these extraordinary proceedings Richard set before himself
the attainment of a great prize — the duchy of Lancaster
itself. No doubt, if he had already at this juncture seen the
possibilities looming ahead, he considered that six years
would suffice as well as ten for the period during which
Henry should be out of the realm. But as it turned out, six
months was long enough. Henry himself foresaw that
probably his father, John of Gaunt, already failing in
health, might not survive much longer, even without the
shock and disgrace of the recent turn of events. He therefore prudently sought and obtained from Richard on 8
October, 1398, letters patent authorizing him to appoint
lawful attornies to receive on his behalf any inheritances of
property that might fall to him during his absence abroad,
and on 13 October he departed the realm.

As early as 3 February, 1399, 'old John of Gaunt' gave
up the ghost, and now nothing (or so it seemed) stood

Richard II

Tomb-effigy in Westminster Abbey. Possibly completed in
1395.

between Richard and the inheritance of Lancaster but the
royal letters patent of 8 October. Of the family of Edward
III there was none left in the realm who could or would
restrain him, certainly not his sole surviving uncle, Edmund
of Langley and of York, too timid and ineffectual to have
any influence upon his, by this time almost omnipotent,

nephew at the very climax of his triumph over all opponents and opposition.

Modern historians have fathered numerous motives upon Richard II, but unfortunately Richard himself left us no record of the aims which moved him in what followed. We cannot tell what precise thoughts led him to take the fateful, and as it proved, the fatal, decision to reach out and seize the great inheritance of Lancaster. It would indeed most probably be a mistake to suppose that he was moved merely by vindictive motives against his cousin Henry. That he did in fact cherish for many years hopes of revenge for the injuries done to him and his friends by the Appellants in the earlier years of his reign can scarcely be doubted in the light of the actual events. But by 1399 his thirst for revenge must have become largely assuaged, and although no doubt a measure of personal animosity entered into his frame of mind at the time, the issues involved were too weighty to be thought of in terms of personal spite alone. There was high policy to be thought of as well. Everyone would agree that whatever else Richard II believed in, he certainly believed in the monarchy — in the personal exercise of the kingship by the monarch himself. The career of Richard II has no meaning at all except in terms of the resurrection of the personal monarchy which had fallen into decline and jeopardy since the last years of his grandfather Edward III. Since a resurrection of this kind is precisely what was achieved by Henry VII a hundred years later, we can scarcely deny that if Richard II had succeeded as Henry VII succeeded, his later reputation would have been very different from what it was, and most likely we should never have heard of Henry VII and the 'foundations of the Tudor monarchy' at all.

Richard may well have looked about him before he acted; his personal and bitter experience of the weakness of a young king confronted by over-mighty uncles and magnates must indeed have sharpened his wits and his perceptions. He must have realized the inevitable menace to the Crown and the peace of the realm in the future arising from the existence of the great duchy with its widespread tentacles, its wealth in men and resources, and its palatine privileges. The rashness of Edward III in allowing the growth of this 'kingdom within the kingdom' was not so apparent so long as the kinglet, John of Gaunt, in his wiser and mellower years was disposed to support the king as a loyal uncle should. But what was the future to be, when John gave way to his son Henry? Henry's record of martial ardour, impetuosity, ambition, and dubious attitudes towards the Crown and towards the king — his equal in age if not in guile, but devoid of any heir apparent to stabilize the dynasty, could hardly inspire confidence. The means to extinguish the independence of the dangerous duchy seemed now so easy and ready to hand, no matter how outrageous the outcome, that it is not surprising that Richard grasped them. He sought to annex the duchy of Lancaster to the Crown. This aim in fact was to be permanently achieved, not indeed by Richard, but by Henry himself. The Crown sought to grasp Lancaster; instead Lancaster grasped the Crown.

The means which Richard found to hand in early 1399 were fatally easy. It was easy to insert an amendment to the record of the terms of reference for the parliamentary committee of 1398 so as to cover a little more unfinished business — or rather business not even begun — and thereafter with the committee's connivance on 18 March solemnly to revoke the letters patent of 8 October on the grounds that they had been issued by 'a mistake'; easy enough to extend the term of Henry's banishment to that of his natural life, and then to confiscate to the king the inheritance of Lancaster. The legal formalities completed, there was nothing to stop Richard from seeking to placate a number of his noble supporters by granting away to them

D

portions of the Lancastrian lands, whilst decently providing for the continued payment of annuities which had been granted by John of Gaunt. If only cousin Henry had acquiesced, had suddenly died, or had gone further afield (he had not got beyond Paris), it is most probable that Richard II would have succeeded as Henry VIII after him succeeded in much greater projects of confiscation. But Henry Bolingbroke was no defenceless abbot or prior, and instead of going further afield, he came home — whilst Richard, secure as he thought in the hour of his greatest triumph, set out to Ireland to avenge another and potentially dangerous injury — the slaughter of his lieutenant and heir presumptive, Roger Mortimer — leaving that man of straw, his uncle Edmund of Langley and York, as the 'guardian' of the realm.

We cannot tell with just what expectation Henry landed on a judiciously chosen parcel of Lancastrian land on the Yorkshire coast near Ravenspur about 4 July. He gave out that all he wanted was his lawful inheritance, but the thought cannot have been far from his mind that even if he got it, he was not likely to enjoy it very long whilst Richard remained king. But even Henry can hardly have imagined that he himself would actually have become unquestionably *de facto* king of England, titular king of France, lord of Ireland, and *de jure* duke of Lancaster, by October of the same year.

The unexpected fact was that the régime of Richard II collapsed with scarcely a show of resistance. For one thing, Richard's guardian of the realm — uncle Edmund — betrayed his trust first by doing nothing effective and then by deciding within a month to throw in his lot with his Lancastrian nephew and seeing what came of it. For another thing, Henry found himself not without powerful friends, or at least allies, who were willing enough to try their hands at coercing Richard. He had also brought back with him from exile the shrewd and experienced counsellor, Thomas Arundel, the archiepiscopal brother of the late

*Henry Bolingbroke, earl of Derby, duke of Hereford
and Lancaster, escorts Richard II to London, 1399*

(*The Deposition and Death of Richard II*, attributed to Créton,
B.M. Harleian MS. 1319, fo. 53b)

Appellant earl of Arundel, and also the latter's son and
heir-hopeful. Moreover, he was soon joined by the powerful earls of Northumberland and Westmorland, by
Northumberland's fire-brand son Harry Hotspur, and
other war-like northern lords; he could count on the help of
many of the Lancastrian tenants, and upon the neutrality
of the vast bulk of the population who had no great
enthusiasm for Richard II (whilst he remained king).
Rapid organization and marching brought him and his
forces to Berkeley Castle by 27 July, and to Chester by 9
August. But his best friends were time and chance. For the
news of these events was delayed in reaching Richard II in
Ireland, and he could not get back soon enough to prevent

Richard II yields the Crown to Henry Bolingbroke, 1399

(Froissart's *Chroniques*, B.M. Harleian MS. 4380, fo. 184b)

himself from being pent up in Wales, deprived of the forces which had there awaited him but which could not be kept together long enough to give him strength when he did arrive. He was still able to reach, with a few followers, the impregnable fortress of Conway Castle, with an easy way of escape still available to him by sea. But he did not take this last chance; he preferred, it seems, to accept the word of his cousin Henry that his person and Crown would be unharmed, and perhaps he still cherished hopes of a final revenge. It is, in all the circumstances, extraordinary that he should have been so trusting and optimistic. Perhaps it was more in keeping with his high sense of royal dignity that he should have agreed to travel towards Flint rather than board a ship and roam abroad, a king without a kingdom. He did not foresee that he would be made prisoner on the way, and would never again be free so long as he lived — which would not be very long.

We need not here trace in detail the procedure of usurpation; how Henry persuaded Richard to abdicate 'voluntarily' on 29 September; how the abdication was accepted and a deposition pronounced by a 'committee' of the members and lords of the parliament which had been summoned in Richard's name for 30 September but which no one now ventured to call a lawful parliament; how Henry stepped forward and claimed the Crown by right of descent of the right line from Henry III (so he said), by his 'recovery' of it when it was on the point of ruin by misgovernance and the decay of good laws; nor how this claim, which avoided all pretence of a parliamentary title, was accepted. But no one can deny, whatever Richard II's trespasses may have been, the extreme poignancy of his last recorded words. After all duty of obedience to him had been repudiated, 'he looked not thereafter', he said, 'but that after all this he hoped that his cousin would be good lord to him'.

The best that Henry could do was to condemn him to secret imprisonment for life. Perhaps he would have spared his life indefinitely, but Richard's best friends proved to be his undoing. Insurrections in his favour early in the following year brought him a final release from his troubles, in the Lancastrian castle of Pontefract, as the result of arrangements made by his jailer, none other than Sir Thomas Swynford, son of John of Gaunt's third wife by her first husband, who thus did his bit to ensure the future for Lancaster. For Richard honourable interment in Westminster Abbey followed, in February, 1400. With the last male Plantagenet of the senior line gone, and the heir presumptive (Edmund Mortimer II, earl of March) a mere child, King Henry IV could plausibly persuade himself that the House of Lancaster was firmly enthroned — and so it was, for sixty years.

But the thirteen years of Henry IV's reign were to prove no primrose path. The strains and stresses of retaining the position which he had won, of coping with malcontents, rebels, and refractory parliaments, of procuring the financial support required for his government, of trying to hand on the Crown to his son and heir, were to be very great, and combined in the end with his failing health brought him to an uneasy death-bed at the age of forty-six.

It was inevitable that a usurpation such as Henry IV managed to accomplish, no matter how hard he should strive (as strive he did) to maintain all the prerogative and powers of the Crown, would result in a weakening of the kingship. Subjects tending to be over-mighty could now view the king as little more than one of themselves grown big and upstart; turbulent spirits, English, Welsh, and Scots, could try what force might do to improve their fortunes; the Commons in parliaments, even if they were willing enough to declare that Henry IV was possessed of no less regality than his predecessors the kings of England, could take it upon themselves to criticize his government, to reform his methods, and curtail his expenditure by withholding money grants or by assenting to them only upon conditions. Finance was to prove in the long run one of the greatest stumbling-blocks in the path of the permanence of the Lancastrian dynasty, and a prime cause of its ultimate failure.

Henry IV, did, however, contrive to deal successfully with the series of armed insurrections with which he was confronted. His military skill and ruthless energy when aroused stood him in good stead. His popularity with the common people, which did not fade too soon, helped him out in the first year of his reign. The magnate leaders of the first of the insurrections, intended to be favourable to, but actually fatal to, Richard, were obligingly done to death by the mobs of Cirencester, Pleshy, and Bristol, and a Bloody Assize at Oxford disposed of a couple of dozen or so of the lesser insurgents.

Scotland could be kept quiet for a time by a short sharp expedition led by Henry IV himself — the last ever to be led into Scotland by a king of England in person. A Scots retaliation met with disaster at Homildon Hill in 1402 at the hands of the earl of Northumberland and the other Percys, and this advantage over Scotland was amply confirmed by the capture at sea of James, the heir of the king of Scots, in 1406. It was during his protracted sojourn at Windsor that the future King James I's poetic vein and matrimonial intents alike were captivated by the charms of Joan Beaufort, the grand-daughter of John of Gaunt through his first Beaufort son. The House of Lancaster thereafter had little difficulty with Scotland — until the time came when in February, 1437, Katherine Douglas should have cause to break her arm trying in vain to bar the door of Queen Joan's bedchamber against her husband's murderers.

More troublesome to Henry IV were the Percy family

and their associates in the northern parts, the activities of the surviving uncle (Sir Edmund Mortimer) of Richard II's heir presumptive Edmund Mortimer II, earl of March, and the co-operation of all of them with that perpetual thorn in Henry IV's western flank, the self-styled prince of Wales, Owen Glendower.

The first phase of these difficulties came to an end with Henry's resounding victory at the battle of Shrewsbury on 21 July, 1403. A number of curious circumstances combined to produce that culmination. Henry Percy, first earl of Northumberland, had lost no time in lending his powerful — probably decisive — support to Henry Bolingbroke in the summer of 1399, doubtless in the expectation of favours to come should Bolingbroke become king, or even merely duke of Lancaster. But the Percys did not get as much as they hoped out of the turn of events, and even their valuable services at Homildon Hill brought them little more than a rebuff in the form of a prohibition (contrary to custom) upon their recuperating expenses by ransoming some of their more affluent Scots prisoners.

But worse things were to follow. Northumberland's fiery son, Harry Hotspur, had married into the Mortimer family. His wife was none other than an aunt of Richard II's last heir presumptive, and a situation of grave possibilities ensued when her brother, Sir Edmund Mortimer, was captured by the Welsh insurgent Owen Glendower in June, 1402. No doubt Henry IV was not sorry to hear that the senior male Mortimer was no longer at liberty, but it was extremely tactless of him to go so far as to refuse to allow him to be ransomed in accordance with custom. Such an attitude could not fail to offend not only Mortimer, but also his brother-in-law, the already dissatisfied Hotspur, with his formidable father of Northumberland behind him. Sir Edmund soon discovered compensations for the blows of fortune. A daughter of Owen Glendower found favour in his eyes, and he even went so far as to marry her. With Glendower as father-in-law, Hotspur as brother-in-law, and Richard II's heir presumptive as nephew, and with a few war-like Scots languishing un-ransomed in the earl of Northumberland's custody, the heady wine of aggrieved ambition went to Sir Edmund's head. Few more fantastic episodes have occurred in English history than the concoction a short time later of the preposterous Treaty of Partition, whereby Wales and the Marches were to go to Glendower, the northern half of England to the Percys, and the southern half to Mortimer.

Henry IV was too quick for the conspirators, too quick even for the impetuosity of Harry Hotspur, who, together with his uncle Thomas Percy, earl of Worcester (who was at the time actually the king's own steward of the House-hold), and the Scots captive earl of Douglas, found their way to a juncture with Glendower barred at Shrewsbury by Henry IV in person and his son Harry of Monmouth, then fifteen years old. When the desperate fight was over, Hotspur was dead, Worcester available for execution, and Douglas the king's prisoner. Henry IV's very speed saved the earl of Northumberland, who had not had time to join his son before Shrewsbury. He managed to avoid a judg-ment of treason by the lords in the parliament of 1404, but was found guilty of trespass. He was nominally forgiven by Henry IV, and lived to try again another day.

That day was not long in coming. In April, 1405, Northumberland attacked Ralph Neville, first earl of Westmorland, whom Henry IV had recently made Warden of the West Marches towards Scotland, renewed his wonderful Treaty of Partition with Sir Edmund Mortimer and Glendower, and by May was in open revolt in the north, and in strange company. He was joined by Thomas Mowbray (the aggrieved son of Henry IV's old antag-onist), by a minor baron, Lord Bardolf, and by no less a person than Richard Scrope, archbishop of York, whose manifesto of simple home-truths must have been singularly unpalatable to Henry IV, coming as it did from the man who had sat on his left hand at his coronation banquet. At Shipton Moor, Mowbray and Scrope capitulated, victims of the guile of the earl of Westmorland and the king's third son, John, and soon found themselves in that useful Lancastrian stronghold, Pontefract Castle, to await the king's own arrival. By now, Henry IV's blood was up; he would not brook delay in getting the heads off the shoulders of both Mowbray and Scrope, and heeded not the expostulations of Thomas Arundel of Canterbury, who rode up by day and night to try to save his archiepiscopal brother. The prelate's head fell, but Henry's throne did not. His arch-enemy, Henry Percy, earl of Northumberland, with Lord Bardolf and others, found their way to an uneasy refuge in Scotland, and it was not until February, 1408, that Henry Percy's schemes were brought to nought at Bramham Moor and his head rested on a sharp pale on London Bridge.

Henry IV had triumphed over all his enemies at home, and could leave to the growing martial ardour and skill of his son Harry of Monmouth the gradual reduction of Glendower to the status of a fugitive, finally to be admitted to pardon and grace in the year of Agincourt. Henry IV had grasped the Crown, and in spite of all kept it to hand over to his son peaceably enough when the end for him came on 20 March, 1413. Whether he was ever able to reconcile his career with his conscience we must leave to speculation. Any doubts he may have entertained at the last, were not, it seems, in any degree shared by his son and heir.

By Mary of Bohun, his first wife, Henry IV had had four sons and two daughters. His second wife, Johanna of Navarre, who survived him by twenty years, made no additions to his family. His eldest son, Henry, was born in 1387, at Monmouth Castle (then part of the duchy of Lancaster estates), and was followed in due course by

Henry IV

(Enlargement of figure in the initial letter of P.R.O. *The Great Cowchers of the duchy of Lancaster,* vol. I, fo. 51)

Thomas, later duke of Clarence; John, later duke of Bedford; and by Humphrey, later duke of Gloucester. With four stalwart sons all growing to manhood before 1399, it must have seemed to Henry of Bolingbroke that his dynasty would not easily come to grief for lack of male heirs. But in fact all his sons were dead by 1435 without a

An early fifteenth-century patron and artist:
John, Lord Lovell of Tichmersh (d. 1408) and
Brother John Siterwas

(A Lectionary c. 1400, B.M. Harleian MS. 7026, fo. 1b)

son or even a daughter left behind any of them, except only Harry of Monmouth's weakling boy, who by then had reached his fourteenth year. Even the impregnable self-confidence of Harry of Monmouth himself would surely have been shaken if he could have known that harsh fact. But such alarming visions were hidden from him, and it was his lot to bring the fortunes of Lancaster to their highest point of triumph. His father had added the Crown of England to the duchy; it remained for him to add to both the Crown of France — if he could. He could and did — or so he thought.

When Henry V succeeded to the throne, at the age of twenty-six, with a good deal of military training and experience in England and Wales, and a little and not very happy experience of government behind him, he was very much better provided with relatives keenly interested in the maintenance of the dynasty and sufficiently matured, or soon to be, to lend security, than his two predecessors had been. He had no 'wicked uncles'; indeed he had no uncles at all living in 1413, except Edward, duke of York (who was to die without lineal heir at Agincourt), and except the two surviving Beaufort half-uncles, Bishop Henry and Thomas, earl of Dorset since 1411 and soon to be duke of Exeter, both of whom were ready enough with wise counsel or naval and military prowess to support their royal kinsman. He could count on the loyalty of his three brothers; his Beaufort 'half-cousins' were as yet too young to count; and so were his cousins of Stafford and Bourchier. His 'half-aunt' Joan Beaufort had married as her second husband the redoubtable and reliable Ralph Neville, first earl of Westmorland, and was busily engaged in providing him with a further nine children to add to the seven he already had. No one as yet could imagine that his sixteenth child would become the mother of a rival dynasty of York.

The only dynastic trouble that came to Henry V arose from the younger line of his great-uncle Edmund of York, whose ineffectual guardianship of the realm in 1399 had contributed so much to Henry IV's initial advantage. Edmund had left two sons; Edward, second duke of York, who was to share the death of warriors at Agincourt, and Richard of Conisburgh. Richard, just created earl of Cambridge by Henry V, saw a greater future for himself if only his first wife's (Anne Mortimer's) brother, Edmund Mortimer II, earl of March, Richard II's heir presumptive, could be substituted for Henry V. Should Edmund Mortimer not want to play, then a pseudo-Richard II would do. But not only would Edmund not play; he would not even refrain from informing Henry V of the plot. At that time the king was about to set out on his first expedition to France, which accounts for the fact that it was outside the north gate of Southampton that Richard of Cambridge lost his head, after due though rapid trial by a tribunal of his peers.

An unpleasant episode this must have been to Henry V, but not unduly disturbing. It was at best a far-fetched and feckless plot, a last flicker of the Mortimer spectre rather than the first presage of the Yorkist nightmare. There was indeed no genuine Yorkist colour to it. Richard of Cambridge's and Anne Mortimer's boy (the duke of York of the future) was as yet only two or three years of age, much too young to meditate upon his descent from two of the sons of Edward III.

Henry V at any rate was not to be deterred from proceeding at once with the great and all-consuming objective of his life — the conquest of France. We shall never know just what circumstances induced him to revive his great-grandfather's hopes and aspirations in that direction. He was not subject to any immediate provocation. The matter of France had been largely quiescent for several decades. Richard II had actually married a daughter of the king of

Henry V

(B.M. Cottonian MS. Julius E IV, fo. 7b. The pictures of the
kings of England, of which this is one, contained in the first
part of this MS. were probably completed early in the reign
of Henry VI.)

France; Henry IV had been too preoccupied at home to worry much about the relics of the Angevin empire. It is possible, though not perhaps probable, that Henry V deliberately determined upon a policy of foreign adventure as a means of securing unity and popular support at home, and as a channel for the diversion of magnate energies and ambitions. The crucial fact was that the course of events in France itself had opened up prospects far more tempting than any that had confronted Edward III. France had become divided against herself, and Henry V had become very well aware of the opportunities which this situation offered, from his own brief personal experience of government in the last four years of his father's reign. The weakness of France in the early years of the fifteenth century may indeed have saved the situation for Lancaster at home, for Henry IV could hardly have coped with much aggression from that quarter. The insanity of Charles VI of Valois may have helped at that time to preserve the Lancastrian dynasty, but in the long run was to bring disaster, for it proved to be congenital, and was to reappear with momentous consequences in Charles VI's grandson, Henry V's own son. Henry V did not, in the eager fulfilment of his designs, reckon with the far-reaching power of hereditary disease.

With the throne of France occupied from 1392 by a mental defective, a struggle for ascendancy between the two rival branches of the royal family — of Orléans (or Armagnac) and of Burgundy ensued, and assumed the character of a blood-feud after the murder of Louis, duke of Orléans, in 1407. Each faction in these circumstances did not scruple to seek the aid of Henry IV. At the time Henry IV himself was in failing health, and the government was dominated by his son, who in 1411 anticipated the policy on which later he was to thrive, by making an alliance with Burgundy. But this policy was reversed a year later when Prince Henry had to give way to Arch-

Charles, duke of Orléans, in the Tower of London,
1415–1440

(*Poems*, etc., B.M. Royal MS. 16 F II, fo. 173)

bishop Arundel's ascendancy, and an alliance with
Armagnac was substituted in exchange for the offer of a
restoration of Acquitaine. Nothing material resulted from
these tergiversations, but none the less the way had been
pointed out to Henry V.

We cannot here trace the course of Henry V's campaigns

E

in France, not even the first campaign culminating in the
superb military feat of arms at Agincourt on 25 October,
1415, which raised the prestige of Lancaster and his 'band
of brothers' to its peak, and restored England once more to
the foremost place among European military powers. It
was Crécy and Poitiers all over again — and in more
senses than one. The conquest of France still remained to
be accomplished. Normandy could be, and was, overrun
during the next two years, and the way to Paris opened up.
But Burgundy held aloof and would not aid the English
invaders, until once again the French blood-feud forced
the pace. At the Bridge of Montereau on 26 August, 1419,
John the Fearless, duke of Burgundy, who at any rate had
not feared to set the precedent by instigating the murder of
Louis of Orléans in 1407, was done to death by men whose
memories were longer than their sense of political realities
was strong. Burgundy's son and heir, Philip the Good, at
once concluded an active alliance with the victor of
Agincourt. Within a year, Henry V was able to impose
upon the Queen of France and other representatives of
Charles VI (but not his son the Dauphin) the Treaty of
Troyes, whereby it was agreed that he should marry
Charles VI's daughter Katherine, rule France (if he could)
in the name of his father-in-law, and should succeed him
as king of France in the event (not likely to be long
delayed) of his father-in-law's release from earthly travail.
The extraordinary turn of events had brought the heir of
Lancaster and Plantagenet to the inheritance of the Valois.

But it was easier to implement the first part of the Treaty
than the other two parts. Henry could marry Katherine on
2 June, 1420, and bring his Queen (and unbeknown to him
a future wife for one Owen Tudor), to England, and beget
a son, Henry, born 6 December, 1421 (destined to be the
only man ever to be crowned king of England and of
France), but in less than a year from then Henry V was
obliged to assume a celestial crown in place of all terrestrial

*Katherine Valois, widow of Henry V,
and wife of Owen Tudor (d. 1437)*

Funeral effigy in Westminster Abbey

ones. The last of the medieval warrior-kings of England,
austere in life, single-minded in purpose, a pattern of
chivalry, he had lived and conquered by the sword, the
greatest of his House; but natural causes laid him low
before the walls of Vincennes on 31 August, 1422. His
dreams lived on, to bedevil his successor, his House, and
his realm for decades thereafter. It was hardly to be
expected that the dynasty would indefinitely survive the
wreckage of its boldest enterprise.

Certainly the premature death of Henry V was the first
irremediable blow to the fortunes of Lancaster. The heir
and new king of England and titular heir of France was a
baby of nine months. His mother Katherine was an
inexperienced girl of twenty-one who had had an unhappy
childhood, had been nurtured in a convent, was totally
ignorant of affairs of state, and was hardly known in
England. She was to count for nothing in the politics of the
time and practically for nothing in the upbringing of her
son, whose tutelage was committed first to Thomas
Beaufort, duke of Exeter, and after 1427 to Richard
Beauchamp, earl of Warwick, son of that Thomas
Beauchamp whom Henry IV had liberated from the Isle
of Man in 1399. There was no lack of both elderly and
young relatives to watch over Henry VI's (and their own)
interests. His eldest uncle, Thomas, duke of Clarence was
indeed lost to him, having been killed at Beaugé in 1421.
The next uncle, John, duke of Bedford, survived to render
yeoman service, and to be a steadfast heir presumptive
until his death in 1435. The youngest uncle, Humphrey,
duke of Gloucester, turbulent, volatile, and assertive,
could consider himself next heir presumptive until his
death without heir in 1447. In that same year, Henry
Beaufort, bishop and cardinal, the only surviving Beaufort
of the first generation after the death twenty years before
of his brother Thomas, duke of Exeter, departed the scene
of his earthly ambitions. The second generation of male

Beauforts had come forward, but by the same year 1447 only one of them was left alive. Henry Beaufort I, earl of Somerset, died young without issue; John Beaufort II, earl and duke of Somerset, had died in 1444, leaving only a daughter, Margaret, still too young even for the first of her matrimonial ventures. By 1447, therefore, the heirship presumptive seemed to have come to the surviving Edmund Beaufort I, earl and marquis of Dorset and duke of Somerset. The defence of Lancaster would largely fall to him, if the time were to come when defence were needed, aided by the stalwart cousins of Stafford. The cousins of Bourchier might take a different view of the question of the ultimate succession, in consequence of matrimonial connexions of their own; for Henry Bourchier, Viscount Bourchier, earl of Essex, married Isabel, the sister of no less a person than Richard, duke of York.

With the accession of a king so young as Henry VI, the problem of government was bound to be acute. The Council of magnates came into its own and ruled the roost for many years as best it could. It had to set up a Protectorate of some kind, and as Protector they preferred to have John, duke of Bedford, and would have as little as possible to do with the pretensions of Humphrey, duke of Gloucester. But Bedford deemed his primary duty to be to carry on as Regent of France on his nephew's behalf. The best compromise they could make was to arrange for Bedford to be the Protector automatically whenever he came to England, whilst Gloucester should hold the office otherwise, but with as little personal power as possible. He did not like that at all, was truculent and refractory, but was forced to abide by the Council's decision. For more than a decade the government of England was conciliar in form and fact. The squabbles and recriminations between Humphrey and Bishop Beaufort, the other most prominent councillor, and the interventions from time to time of John of Bedford, need not detain us here.

John, duke of Bedford, kneels before St. George

(*Book of Hours*, B.M. Add. MS. 18,850, fo. 256b. This book
was executed for the duke and duchess of Bedford and presented to Henry VI on Christmas eve at Rouen, 1430, when
he was *en route* to be crowned king of France.)

Henry VI was not regarded as of age until 1437, and the government until then was necessarily carried on in his name. The Council, despite the difficulties arising from rival personalities and the inherent tendency of magnates to prefer self-interests to public policy whilst leaving the real work to the principal officers, contrived to improve itself as an administrative organ, and to maintain a fair degree of stability, but its efforts were not blessed with much success in matters of major policy, least of all in the matter of France. The death of Charles VI on 21 October, 1422, brought an early proclamation of Henry VI as king of France in accordance with the Treaty of Troyes. But it was easier to make proclamations than to make headway, and despite the whole-hearted efforts of John of Bedford, and some successes gained by him in the early years of the minority, the odds were against the fulfilment in reality of Henry V's dreams. For one thing, John soon had to contend with a growing lack of enthusiasm on the part of the duke of Burgundy, without whose active co-operation any ultimate success was improbable, if not indeed impossible. Whatever heart-searchings Burgundy may have had about the justification for his policy, his personal feelings were enraged by the matrimonial ventures of, curiously enough, both Humphrey and John. Humphrey's entanglement with Countess Jacqueline of Hainault in the life-time of her husband the count, and his quixotic attempt to add possession of the territory of Hainault to that of the countess's person, gave great offence to Burgundy, the count's overlord, and it took all of John of Bedford's diplomatic patience to prevent a complete rupture. Then the time came when the staid and cautious John himself committed a matrimonial indiscretion which further annoyed Burgundy. John had, as part of a treaty of alliance with him, and before the Humphrey-Jacqueline affair blew up, married in 1423 at the age of thirty-four one of the duke's sisters, Ann, and no doubt hoped by such

Ann, duchess of Bedford, kneels before the Virgin
(*Book of Hours*, B.M. Add. MS. 18,850, fo. 257b)

means to ensure the security of the alliance between the two countries; and so it did, for a time. But in 1432, the gracious and greatly beloved Ann (who had dared to show kindness to *La Pucelle*) died. Within a year, Bedford, now aged forty-four, resolved to marry an attractive girl of seventeen, one Jacquetta, daughter of Peter, count of St Pol, and niece of John of Luxembourg, who was Burgundy's chief captain — without so much as consulting the duke himself. Bedford could not be expected to realize that in bringing Jacquetta to England he was providing the future Edward IV with a mother-in-law, but he should have paid more heed to the alliance with Burgundy, which was very soon to be brought to an abrupt end.

In the meantime there had occurred another and even more disturbing course of events. Joan of Arc had heard her 'voices' and fulfilled her mission; she had made her journey to Chinon; had convinced Dauphin Charles of his legitimacy; had appeared in shining armour at the relief of Orléans and at the battle of Patay; had knelt beside Charles at his coronation in the cathedral of Rheims; had assaulted (in vain) the walls of Paris; had been captured at Compiègne by the Burgundians and sold to the English; had been tried, convicted, and condemned to death as a relapsed heretic by an ecclesiastical court; and had, in the market square of Rouen on 30 May, 1431, been burnt to ashes which were carefully collected and thrown into the Seine.

With the last traces of Joan's body floating away to oblivion — or so it seemed — it was practicable for Regent Bedford to get his nephew Henry VI, now nine years old, over to Paris and to have him hallowed in Notre Dame by his uncle Bishop Beaufort, now cardinal, and crowned king of France, by 16 December. But France herself was not there.

Nor was Burgundy either. On 8 September, Philip of Burgundy had signed a two years' truce with his liege lord

Charles VII. Within four years it was all over with the Anglo-Burgundian alliance. From the Congress of Arras the English delegates retired on 6 September, 1435, without having come to any terms with the French, all unaware that the long feud between Burgundians and Armagnacs had already been brought to an end by a secret agreement reached by Duke Philip and Charles VII. Within ten days thereafter, the much harassed Regent John of Bedford himself was dead, and with him died the chance that the Will of Henry V, whose principal executor he had been, would ever be carried out.

By 1437, Henry VI was reckoned to have come of age, and in the the same year two minor revelations were made, of little more than scandalous interest at the time but of great consequence in the long run. On 23 March, Jacquetta, the widow of John of Bedford, was permitted to compound for the offence she had committed in marrying without leave one of her late husband's household, Sir Richard Woodville. The future thirteen Woodville children were thus provided with their parents, but nobody cared much — then. On 26 March, administrators were appointed to execute the Last Will and Testament of Katherine of Valois, the almost-forgotten widow of Henry V. It could no longer be concealed that for some years she had been consoling herself with a young, handsome, and personable Welsh clerk of her Wardrobe, by the name of Owen Tudor. She had not only, in the eyes of the Church, married him (whether she was in a position to do so in the eyes of secular society is another and more doubtful matter), but had also borne him three sons and a daughter. Their youngest son and the daughter were not destined to make any impression upon history, but Edmund and Jasper Tudor were now firmly on the scene, and were not going to be neglected by their ever-benign half-brother, Henry VI.

Benignity, indeed, was to be Henry VI's most charming,

Henry VI

Painting in custody of Ministry of Works. Artist unknown.
Attributed to the Flemish School, c. 1510.

persistent, and disastrous characteristic. Saintliness without a strong head and strong right arm is always a dangerous thing in a king who is expected to govern sinners, and Henry VI possessed neither of the needful accessories but had plenty of ungovernable sinners among his subjects who were glad enough to enjoy their sins under the aegis, so long as it served, of his all-embracing benevolence. The fruits of the sinners' activities have faded away, but the memorial of Henry VI in his noble foundations of Eton College and King's College, Cambridge, is with us still, and so is that of his sorely-tried Queen, even if this had to be refounded by her Woodville successor to form Queens' College, Cambridge.

But poor Henry could not govern, and others perforce had to govern for him. For some years the ascendancy went to his sole surviving uncle of the whole blood, Humphrey of Gloucester, and his great-uncle of the half-blood, Cardinal Beaufort. But Humphrey's lack of stability and lack of heirs tended to promote the influence of the Beaufort interest, all the more as Humphrey led the faction whose policy was 'war with France at any price', whilst the Beauforts tended towards the opposite policy of 'peace with France at all costs', and Henry VI found the latter more congenial to his pacific heart.

The fact that so many years elapsed before any decisive crisis arose argues strongly for the affection in which Henry VI was widely held, the even balance of interests, the comparative restraint of most members of the family of Edward III, and the general reluctance to upset the inheritance of Lancaster, so long as inaction brought only drift, uncertainty, and a gradual decay in fortunes. But by the end of 1453, many things had happened which together brought inescapable crisis.

The personal rivalries of Humphrey of Gloucester and Cardinal Beaufort had come to an end with the death of both of them in 1447. Humphrey, whose ruin by the machinations of his opponents had come to be all but sealed, died probably by natural causes; Beaufort, ripe in years and in at any rate earthly treasure, certainly by natural causes. His death left his nephew, Edmund Beaufort I, duke of Somerset, and the latter's young son Henry, to represent the Beaufort male line.

A new and powerful star in the Beaufort connexion had appeared, risen, run his course, and fallen by 1450. William de la Pole, earl, and since 1448, duke, of Suffolk, a grandson of that Michael de la Pole who had fallen foul of the Lords Appellant in the Merciless Parliament of 1388, figured for some years as the strong man of the Lancastrian-Beaufort party. He had climbed to high repute as a soldier in the French wars under Henry V and John of Bedford. But he had passed over to the 'peace party', as well he might, for he had married, (not indeed the Lady Margaret Beaufort as at one time seemed probable) but the widowed countess of Salisbury, who was a grand-daughter of Geoffrey Chaucer and the great-niece of Katherine Swynford. He was not to know that later on his son John was to marry the sister of the future Yorkist kings, for his own life came to an abrupt and brutal end in 1450. But not before he had skilfully worked the political ruin of that Beaufort *bête-noir*, Humphrey of Gloucester; nor before he had carried the peace policy to the humiliating length of negotiating the marriage of Henry VI to a poor relation of the Queen of France, the young and beautiful Margaret of Anjou, daughter of Réné, whose titles and cultural interests were more impressive than his landed estate. Margaret, poor indeed in marriage portion but mettlesome and lion-hearted in spirit, was married to the king of England on 23 April, 1445. But before long Suffolk was obliged to connive at the restoration to the French of the county of Maine by way of further cementing the alliance and contributing to a permanent peace. Without a rival in the government after the death of the Cardinal, de la Pole

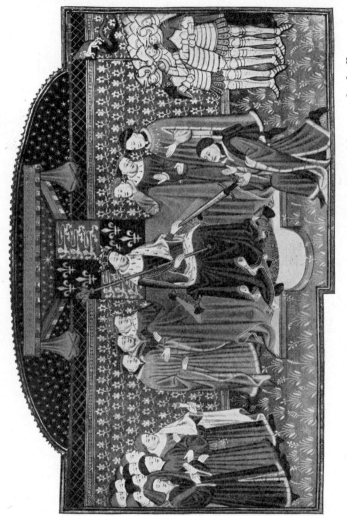

Henry VI hands to John Talbot, earl of Shrewsbury, his sword of office as Constable of France, 1442

(*Poems and Romances in French*, B.M. Royal MS. 15 E. VI, fo. 405)

climbed to marquisate and dukedom and to many offices and great wealth. Almost his first use of his power proved to be a matter of great consequence. He began the process of humiliating and alienating Richard, duke of York, by

Queen Margaret of Anjou

Medal struck in 1463 by Pietro da Milano, Victoria & Albert Museum

then a solid purposeful man of mature years, whose lineage it was best not to talk about, but who was a loyal subject of Henry VI whom he had served manfully even if not very brilliantly as his lieutenant in what remained of the English possessions in France. But now he was supplanted in favour by Edmund Beaufort I, then marquis of Dorset,

John Talbot, earl of Shrewsbury,
presents a book to Queen Margaret of Anjou,
wife of Henry VI, c. 1445

(*Poems and Romances in French*, B.M. Royal MS. 15 E. VI,
fo. 1b)

soon to be duke of Somerset, and relegated to Ireland as
lieutenant there. About that time Richard began to call
himself, on occasions, Richard Plantagenet.

But Suffolk had not lived to see the outcome. His own
extreme unpopularity in the country had brought startling
and ominous events in 1450. The very Commons in
parliament, awaking out of a long political torpor,
sickened and frightened by the long series of losses and
concessions in France, as well as by the flowing tides of
disorder and lawlessness at home, had sought to make
Suffolk the scapegoat. They had 'impeached' him, or tried

to, and when they had failed, they brought in a bill of attainder. To save him from the consequences, and himself from grave and distressing decisions, Henry VI banished him for five years, but only, as it turned out, to expose him to the savagery of the mariners off the Kentish coast. The howl of applause at the ensuing bloody and lawless deed that went up all over the country was symptomatic of the growing deterioration of the public temper. The rebellion of Jack Cade a little later in the year, whether or not it had any Yorkist instigation, had brought the ominous cry once more of 'Mortimer', as well as a manifesto of complaints against the existing government. The noise had reached as far as the duke of York in Ireland, and had induced him to abandon his duties and to force his way into the king's presence unbidden. Edmund of Somerset meantime had been brought home, appointed Constable of England and charged with the task of preparing for eventualities. But Henry VI's own soft answers and kindly demeanour to Richard had staved off overt hostilities, and the royal meekness and conciliatory ways had managed to keep the peace in the parliament of 1450, full though it was with magnates armed and retinued. A rash petition by the member for Bristol for the recognition of the duke of York as heir to the throne brought only dissolution to the parliament and the Tower to the petitioner. Crisis had been postponed; it was not, after all, so easy to browbeat a king as meek and mild as Henry VI.

Richard of York had preferred to direct his onslaught in the direction of Edmund of Somerset, his strongly entrenched rival for the heirship presumptive. He returned to the charge in 1452, but was again foiled, notwithstanding his show of armed force; that episode ended with Somerset still where he had been, and with Richard, as the price of his continued liberty, swearing a solemn oath in public never to do such a thing again. It seemed that a period of quiescence had been reached, and the *status quo* confirmed.

F

Humphrey, duke of Gloucester, and Richard, duke of York

(*Poems and Romances in French*, B.M. Royal MS. 15 E. VI, fo. 3)

But as the year 1453 unfolded, three events occurred which radically changed the situation and irremediably destroyed all hope of stability. On 17 July, the last English long bows were blown out of France (except for Calais) by the gunpowder which the Bureau brothers had brought into the service of the king of France at the battle of Castillon near Bordeaux. The French war was perforce at an end, and there could no longer be any pretence of a show of patriotic unity at home in the face of the common enemy. In the same month, Henry VI's last remaining inheritance from Charles VI caught up with him, and he lost his mental faculties entirely. On 13 October, his Queen Margaret presented him (all unheeding though he was) with a son and heir apparent. Someone now had to be given the reins of government for the duration of the king's incapacity — which might be for the rest of his life. No hope was left now that the better (whoever that might be) of the two possible heirs presumptive might survive to succeed Henry VI when he should pass away (which might be all the sooner because of his illness). No one then could foresee that in fact Henry VI would outlive his own son Edward, Richard of York, Edmund of Somerset, and almost all the male family of his generation, and indeed survive for another eighteen years. But whosoever could become Protector meantime could expect to be able to do much to protect not only the realm but also his own interests.

The struggle between Lancaster and York for both immediate and prospective power had begun, and was to bring intermittent civil war in its train for more than thirty years. It was the Valois dilemma enacted all over again, but fortunately in England there was to be no appreciable interference from abroad. Months passed before either side could make decisive headway. Somerset was obliged to retire to the Tower for a time to avoid the consequences of an 'impeachment' in the parliament of November 1453;

in March 1454, the Lancastrians gained their point that Prince Edward should be created prince of Wales and earl of Chester; the lords in the parliament were still largely Lancastrian in sentiment, but after prolonged hesitation they at last agreed to appoint Richard of York Protector and Defender of the realm in much the same fashion as Humphrey of Gloucester had been appointed thirty-two years before — but only to hold office as long as the king pleased or until the prince of Wales should come of age. Their reluctance and apprehensions are amply testified by the fact that at the same time as York was appointed, a patent was sealed actually nominating the prince as Protector the moment he should attain years of discretion.

York was now entrenched, with Somerset in the Tower pending a problematical trial, and with Exeter under arrest and detained at Pontefract. He could proceed to make appointments to important offices from among his friends. But about Christmastide in 1454, Henry VI suddenly recovered his senses, and was most surprised to learn that he had become a father. York could do no other than give up the Protectorate, whereupon Margaret, resolute and vigorous in giving support to both her husband and her son, set about procuring a reversal of the recent trend. Somerset was freed and all charges against him dropped; Exeter was liberated; York was deprived of the Captaincy of Calais in favour of Somerset's restoration, and his appointments to offices were superseded.

The resulting menace to the Yorkists proved to be too much for the duke to accept; he resorted to arms, and on 22 May, 1455, the first battle of St Albans took place, and ended in his triumph. Somerset was killed in the fighting, along with several other Lancastrian lords, including the heir of Henry Stafford, duke of Buckingham. The English blood-feud had begun, and was not to be appeased for several generations.

Henry VI was escorted politely from the fringe of the

field (where he had sustained a slight wound), and taken to London. But York had gone too far and too fast; popular feeling was critical of his conduct and he could get little from the parliamentary proceedings that followed, except a general pardon for all that he had done before 9 July.

Then in November, under political pressure,[1] a Protectorate was again established, and nothing could stop York from again becoming Protector, notwithstanding the embarrassment and reluctance of the assembled lords. He was not, however, able to make much headway, for by the following January the Protectorate lapsed. Henry VI himself showed signs of being willing to allow York to bear the burdens of government on his behalf, but Margaret and the Lancastrian lords would not hear of that, and he was dismissed on 25 February.

The chastening experiences of all the parties during these last few months helped to produce a lull for more than half a year. Already, however, in 1455, Richard Neville, earl of Warwick, who had sprung into prominence as a Yorkist warrior at St Albans, had been permitted to take an important step forward in what was to be his career as a maker and unmaker of kings by being given the command at Calais. He experienced difficulties for a year in making his command effective, but a key position was thereby secured for the Yorkists. From there he greatly added to his popular reputation and to Yorkist prestige by scoring a somewhat cheap and certainly a buccaneering victory over a squadron of Spanish ships in May 1458. In the meantime occasion had been taken for the staging at home of a wonderful scene of reconciliation, forgiveness, and general amity (objects so dear to Henry VI's innocent

---

[1] It can no longer be maintained that Henry VI was 'again insane', as Stubbs thought. See J. R. Lander, 'Henry VI and the Duke of York's Second Protectorate, 1455 to 1456' in *Bulletin of The John Rylands Library*, vol. 43 (1960).

heart), with the angelic king marching crowned in procession to St Paul's, preceded by the new Somerset walking
hand in hand with Salisbury, Exeter hand in hand with
Warwick, and followed by Queen Margaret led by none
other than York himself.

This magnificent gesture speaks volumes for Henry VI's
gracious loving-kindness, and the sort of man that he was
goes far to explain the extraordinary gradualness of the
recourse to extremes. But in all the circumstances, extremes were inevitable, for the irreconcilable could not be
reconciled.

The year 1459 saw recourse to arms by both sides. A
concentration of forces at Ludlow was not prevented by a
clash at Blore Heath on 23 September; the Lancastrian
forces had been mobilized in strength; the king himself,
with his inexhaustible patience, still sought to avoid a
major battle by offering an amnesty on condition of
disarmament. The Yorkist leaders at Ludlow would have
none of it, but they failed to reckon that many in their
camp might prefer to de-camp and get a pardon whilst the
going was still good. The result was that a fight on Ludford
Bridge ended in the rout of the remaining Yorkists, and
the next day (13 October) saw Richard, duke of York, and
his second son, the earl of Rutland, galloping post-haste to
escape into Wales and thence to Ireland, whilst his eldest
son Edward, earl of March, and the earl of Warwick were
similarly seeking refuge at Calais, *via* Devon and Guernsey.
After all, York was still the king's lieutenant in Ireland,
and Warwick still captain of Calais. But they had left
behind them, helpless and defenceless in Ludlow, Cecily,
York's duchess, and her two (as yet) little innocents,
George and Richard.

Lancaster had scored an overwhelming, and as it
seemed, a decisive victory. The parliament at Coventry in
November, heavily Lancastrian in sentiment, ended with
the duke of York, his two eldest sons, and most of the

Richard, duke of York

Statue formerly over the gateway of the Welsh bridge,
Shrewsbury, now affixed to the old Market House. Artist and
date unknown, but some evidence exists to suggest that the
figure was a near-contemporary representation of Richard,
duke of York.

Yorkist leaders, being put under an act of attainder, to which the king assented while still reserving to himself power to show mercy and grace to any of them; it ended also with the very large number of lords present swearing solemn oaths of allegiance to Henry VI as king 'by succession born to reign', of protection for the Queen, and of acceptance of Prince Edward and his future issue as heirs to the Crown.

But the consequences of the attainder could not be fully enforced. York was safe in Ireland, and Warwick in Calais, both excellent bases from which to concert plans. There were no means available for stopping the return and triumphant entry into London of the earls of Warwick, Salisbury, and March, nor for preventing them from marching on to fight at Northampton on 10 July, 1460, nor from returning to London with Henry VI as their prisoner, leaving many Lancastrian lords lying dead where they had fallen on the field. No use now for the Lancastrian defenders of the Tower to hold out any longer; nothing now to prevent the duke of York himself from leaving his refuge in Ireland, marching to Westminster, displaying at last the 'whole arms of England without difference', and with a naked sword borne before him.

He found a parliament already in session, and the Coventry acts of attainder already reversed. He strode in among the lords assembled, with a flourish of trumpets, and advanced towards the vacant throne as if to occupy it, but the dead silence of the assembly inhibited his act of vulgar intrusion. His kinsman Archbishop Bourchier, politely asked him if he wished to see the king. But York said that he knew of no person in the realm who ought not to wait upon him, and retired in dudgeon to intrude himself into the king's own apartment in the Palace, Henry at that time being with the Queen elsewhere. York had thrown over his allegiance and reached out to the throne itself. But Lancaster himself was not there.

His direct action having met with a rebuff, York got his legal advisers to submit to the lords an unequivocal claim to the Crown. His hitherto unmentionable pedigree was now put fairly and squarely before them. His descent from Lionel, duke of Clarence, son of Edward III begotten before John of Gaunt, was made clear, and carried back through Edward I to Henry III, with the lie direct to Henry Bolingbroke's pretence that Edmund Crouchback had been the first-born of the third Henry. Lancaster was now caught in the toils of legitimism.

The lords were confronted with an appalling dilemma. They had but recently renewed oaths of allegiance to Lancaster; three acts of parliament since 1399 had entailed the Crown upon the lineal heirs of Lancaster; Henry VI's descent from Edward III, even though from a younger son than Clarence, was exclusively through males, whereas York's descent from the elder line was only through two females. But York now had the power of the sword to back him up; Lancaster had failed to govern; York might even yet stem the tides of decadence.

The lords sought the king's advice, who told them to go and find objections to York's claim; they sought the advice of the king's justices, who under the leadership of Chief Justice Sir John Fortescue (who was soon to accept poverty and exile — and also to acquire leisure for writing — rather than submit to York) declared that they were the king's judges and had to determine such matters as came before them in the law, between party and party, and in such matters they might not be of counsel. The matter in hand was between the king and the duke, and moreover this matter was so high that it was above the law and their legal learning.

The lords consulted the king's serjeants-at law, who declared that if the matter were too high for the justices, it was too high for them; and so the lords were obliged to make up their own objections in terms of oaths of allegiance

taken and of acts of parliament unrepealed. Richard of
York could not gain his point. But he was strong enough to
impose upon Lancaster what Lancaster had imposed
upon Valois. Richard should succeed Henry as king, and
Prince Edward should be ousted from the succession just
as the Dauphin had been ousted, and Richard should rule
as Protector of England in Henry VI's life-time just as
Henry V had ruled as Regent of France. It was the Treaty
of Troyes all over again, but in England and with no
marriage contract involved.

Henry VI, like Charles VI before, was acquiescent
enough, but Queen Margaret, unlike Queen Isabel was
far from acquiescent; she did not, as the French Queen is
said to have done, declare that her son was only a bastard.
On the contrary, she and the Lancastrian lords brought
the issue to trial by battle at Wakefield on 30 December,
1460. Many Yorkist lords lay stricken when the day was
over, and York obtained his crown at last. But it was only
a paper crown, and his head upon the gate of York city
had no body to support it.

This was the end of Richard, but not of his cause. His
second son Rutland had been stabbed to death after the
battle, but his eldest son Edward, earl of March, was still
very much alive, and was advancing up from the West,
and was able to inflict a defeat at Mortimer's Cross near
Wigmore (the ancestral home of the Mortimers) on
2 February, 1461, upon Jasper Tudor, earl of Pembroke,
and other Lancastrian lords, and to capture Jasper's
father Owen, quite an old man now, whose proud
memories of Queen Katherine flooded in upon his mind
even as the executioner's axe fell upon his neck.

But Queen Margaret and her forces were meanwhile
advancing towards London, and on 17 February inflicted
another defeat upon the Yorkists at the second battle of
St Albans, where Warwick's military prowess was not
much in evidence; in fact he had been obliged to flee to

the camp of Edward of March. It seemed as though final triumph was within the reach of the Lancastrians. But their delay in getting to London proved to be fatal; Edward and Warwick got there first. On 4 March Edward was acclaimed king in Westminster Hall, and then with great speed pursued the retiring Lancastrians northwards, to come up with them at Towton on 29 March. When that day was over, many Lancastrian lords and some Yorkist ones were no more; Henry VI and Margaret were fleeing towards Scotland. The House of Lancaster had fallen.

The Rise of York

THE House of Lancaster had not merely fallen; it had failed; and it fell because it had failed. It had, in 1399, grasped the kingship, but within less than sixty years thereafter it had shown itself unable to perform adequately the duties inherent in the office. It failed to govern. A widespread consciousness that this failure had been demonstrated beyond a doubt accounts for the sudden success of Edward IV. The Yorkist claimant succeeded in replacing Lancaster not because anyone was profoundly moved by theories of legitimist hereditary right, or indeed by any conception of some clearly defined right of succession to the Crown. The fact was that as yet there was no precise legal rule governing the right to the throne. The judges and the lawyers were not merely being evasive when they pronounced that the problem was too high for their learning. They were simply stating correctly that the law of England had not as yet evolved any decisive rules on the point. The lawyers, it is true, were still tending to think of the kingdom as a piece of real property, the succession to which ought to be by the same rules as applied to an estate in fee simple. But even so, there were bound to be difficulties. Title to land might be inherited by an heiress, but not her father's peerage if he had one. That went into abeyance unless and until it was called out in favour of an eventual male heir, or perhaps in favour of the heiress's husband, if she had one. But the kingship could not go into abeyance, and perhaps therefore it could not be conveyed through a woman. It was a question, in 1460, of

balancing an ostensible legitimist claim through two
females against a prescriptive right of possession conveyed
exclusively through males. The matter was further complicated by the fact that if Henry VI and his son were to be
displaced at all, the Beaufort interest demanded consideration. That interest was at the time represented by
Margaret Beaufort, countess of Richmond, and her very
young son Henry, or if females were not to count, by Henry
Beaufort, second duke of Somerset. It might be assumed
(probably correctly enough) that Henry IV could not
legally have excluded the Beauforts from the line of royal
succession once they had been legitimated. There were
diverse precedents in all these matters dating back from
the Norman Conquest and beyond, but nothing decisive.
Ancient precedent in these matters was still too strong to
be broken entirely by mere parliamentary statutes of
Henry IV's time purporting to prescribe the succession.
The hereditary-right element was a very strong factor,
even if it had never been precisely defined in the past; but
the traditions of the right to choose from among the royal
family, and of the right to set aside even the manifest male
heir if he were unsuitable for the duties of kingship, were
extremely powerful factors also. The whole question of the
succession to the throne was too delicate a matter, and too
closely bound up with the safety and good governance of
the realm to be generally considered a matter wholly
suitable for determination by simple parliamentary
enactment. Indeed, none of the succession Acts from
Henry IV to at least the Bill of Rights of 1689 purported to
do more than declare what was already the accomplished
fact in the matter. Even Sir John Fortescue, who wrote
many pamphlets arguing the Lancastrian cause after
Henry VI's displacement, could, to placate Edward IV a
few years later, and with comparative plausibility, refute
his own arguments.

It is no cause for wonder, therefore, that the magnates

and others, in the 1450's, found it so hard to discover any decisive principles upon which to act. The indeterminate character of the current theories helps to explain the extraordinary slowness with which the duke of York unfolded his claim. True, he had to walk very warily so long as Lancastrian power was dominant, but it seems probable that, if only Henry VI had been able to rule with even average competence, the Yorkist claim, no matter what degree of theoretical validity it might be deemed to have, would never have been advanced at all. But once a resolution that Henry VI must be replaced gained ground, it was an impressive theory with which to justify overt action, and the success of the claim, even if only temporary, undoubtedly helped to consolidate legitimist notions for the future. But the many magnates, the gentry, and their men, who fought and risked their lives and all they possessed during the civil wars, did not sacrifice themselves for the sake of uncertain theoretical principles. They chose their sides for the sake of family connexions and interests, on the principle of 'good lordship', perhaps for the sake of simple 'good fellowship', and even, once blood had been drawn, on the immemorial, aboriginal principles of the feud. The extraordinary family history of the numerous descendants of Edward III, with their extremely wide ramifications throughout the then very limited ranks of the peerage, made the civil wars of the period look like the 'Wars of the Lords Temporal', with several Lords Spiritual, because of family connexions, profoundly interested in the result. The prize at stake was, after all, the greatest earthly prize within the reach of any of them — the Crown of England with all the wealth, power, and influence which went with it.

The House of Lancaster had failed to maintain its position both at home and abroad. Henry V had led the realm into a renewal of the French war, and in a few years had brought it enthusiastically within sight of triumph greater than Edward III in his prime had ever achieved, greater than the Angevins themselves had ever imagined possible. He had given to the people of England the sweet taste of comparatively easy conquest — easy, that was, whilst France herself was hopelessly divided, and so long as one French faction was willing to help the English to pick up the ripe fruit. Rich prizes, large fortunes in ransom-monies and plunder were brought back to England and spread far and wide to enrich many an English soldier and his family, high and low, according to his estate and degree. Parliaments frequently granted taxation, many people in all classes of society who had any money to spare, lent it to the king to finance the campaigns and made still more money in the process by being paid back a good deal more than they had lent. It was boom-time so long as things went well, and it is difficult for us, sufficiently familiar as we are with modern warfare not to expect to grow rich on it, to imagine the growing bitterness and disillusionment, combined with a fanatical resolution not to give up and cut the losses, which afflicted so many strata of society during the first thirty years or so of Henry VI's reign. It must, of course, have been obvious from the start that Henry VI himself could not for many years take any part in saving his father's gains in France, and as he slowly grew to manhood, it must also have become increasingly obvious that he was never going to become a warrior-king capable of pushing home his father's powerful thrust. Hopes were not unreasonably pinned for some years upon John, duke of Bedford's abilities to redeem the situation, or at least to hold it firm. But with the defection of Burgundy and Bedford's death in 1435, few outside die-hard anti-French circles can have seriously expected that much more would come out of the French enterprise, though perhaps no one anticipated the catastrophic losses of the following two decades, even if some for political purposes turned a blind eye to the writing on the wall. It is hard for us also to imagine the humiliation of Lancaster when at last there was nothing to show for all the efforts and sacrifices made except Edward III's Calais. With prestige inevitably credit fell also, and lending money to the Lancastrian government by all classes diminished heavily in the decade 1442–52, and still more heavily in the decade 1452–62, most markedly on the part of the country gentry — hitherto the most conspicuous backers of Lancaster and the French enterprise.

Sharp declines in financial credit hit the Lancastrian régime where it hurt most. For it had never succeeded in solving its financial problems. Henry IV, with so slight an experience of financial or estate management as he had had before he usurped the throne, had shown himself an imprudent and incompetent manager of finance. Even the addition of the duchy of Lancaster to the revenue sources of the king had brought very little extra liquid income to the Crown, for all but a small fraction of the substantial duchy revenues were absorbed by the charges and commitments on the duchy itself. He was forced in any event by the circumstances of the usurpation to make inroads on his resources by alienation, grants, and gifts, and with but little profit accruing from forfeitures. He soon found, as Richard II had found, that the hereditary revenues of the Crown and its various perquisites were not enough to defray the expenses of government, especially when one insurrection after another had to be suppressed. The only means of supplementation were by getting parliamentary grants, to which inconvenient and hampering conditions might be applied, or by recourse to borrowing from lenders who would not lend without assurance of very high rates of interest, even though the usury was concealed by Exchequer procedure.

Under Henry V the underlying insolvency of the Crown was hidden during most of the reign by parliamentary and popular enthusiasm, and by general willingness to finance

Chief Justice Sir John Fortescue
Tomb and effigy in Ebrington Church, Gloucestershire

him, once it was clear that he was going to produce results.

The lords of Henry VI's minority, however, soon found that government bankruptcy was not far off. So alarming was the prospect that they went so far in 1433 as to get the then Treasurer to depart from the happy-go-lucky traditional methods in order to make an estimate of the king's revenue and expenditure for a year ahead, only to reveal a large prospective deficit. But no remedy was found, and never was to be found during the Lancastrian régime. It is not surprising that Sir John Fortescue, when about 1470 he tried to analyse the defects of the Lancastrian government as he had known them (and he and many other officials had had plenty of personal experience of the matter in the form of salaries in arrears), put first 'the poverty of the Crown'.

A government which cannot pay its way cannot discharge properly its primary duty of maintaining order and

enforcing the law. Nor can it do that if its agents do not
feel themselves backed adequately by higher authority,
backed strongly enough to enable them to enforce the law
against the interests of the most powerful and recalcitrant
subjects or combinations of subjects. The problem of law
enforcement was not, of course, new in the Lancastrian
period; it was the perennial medieval problem of government. Indeed it is the eternal problem where the actual
executive power of the government is too weak in relation
to refractory subjects who possess the means to evade the
law's enforcement, or where the law itself is inadequate to
meet the exigencies of the times. The Lancastrian period
as a whole was very weak in constructive legislation of any
kind, but the 'old statutes' of Edward I and the tough
common law were there, and the Common Law courts
never ceased to function, according to their lights. But
their methods were slow and cumbersome, full of techni-
calities, greatly exposed to the possibilities of procrastina-
tion and chicanery, and to corrupt influences, especially in
those parts of the land law and the criminal law which
depended for their efficacy upon the impartiality of jurors.
For if jurors could be got at, there was no hope of getting
justice, no matter how reasonable and customary the rules
of law themselves might be; still less hope if, as sometimes
could happen, undue influences were brought to bear
upon the king's justices. The very king's council itself, in
theory so powerful as the repository of the discretion
inherent in the king himself, was but a broken reed when
the councillors had little to fear from the king himself, but
much from each other or the opposing faction.

Moreover, the bonds of society were no longer what they
had been. For a long time past the king could not get his
armies into the field merely by calling out the feudal host,
on the basis of knight-service. No longer was the firmest
social and legal bond the nexus of tenurial obligation
between lords and vassals, with its tentacles spreading

through all the grades of rural society. Edward I's legislation had, unwittingly, loosened not only the rigidity, but also the cohesion, of feudal land law and custom. But bonds and ties and some comprehensible relationships in a society made up of elements of such vastly differing rank, wealth, and influence, there had to be, and they had been found, if found anywhere, in the principle of 'good lordship'. The old feudal gravitation of lesser men around greater men continued, but no longer necessarily on the basis of fiefs, homage, and specified services. It had become increasingly common for persons to enter into agreements, written or unwritten, 'indentured' or otherwise, on no basis other than mutual self-interest or anticipation of self interest. The greater man would promise to be 'good lord', i.e., to use his influence in every way to promote the interests of the lesser man, or if he were very much lesser, to pay his wages and provide livery, or badge, or some such symbol of protection, in return for the lesser man's help and support when needed, or for his service among his 'bodyguard'. In short, the services, whatever they might be, were 'retained', for a term, perhaps of years, perhaps for life, but not necessarily exclusively. The more substantial the lesser man might be, the more useful and possible he might find it to seek several 'good lords', and hope that no extremities of conflicting interest would arise. 'Interest' permeated all society and governed all things from the course of the dynastic civil war itself to the processes of litigation in the local courts. 'Embracery' and 'maintenance', and all the other forms of bringing undue and theoretically illegal influence to bear on litigation, and even on the very government itself, could thrive only where social commitments, complicated and widespread, rested upon one form or another of 'good lordship'. Parliaments might, and did, legislate against one manifestation or another of the phenomena, which it may or may not be appropriate for historians to label 'bastard feudalism', but the fact was that society in the stage to which it had been brought, could not subsist without it. The king himself could not do without it (neither then nor for a long time thereafter). It filled the vacuum left by the poverty and weakness of the executive power and by the lack of any constructive social and political policies. It was at the root of what Fortescue and other contempories called the 'lack of politique reule and governance'. This widely-felt lack was fatal to the House of Lancaster. In 1460, it remained to be seen whether York could do anything to supply what was lacking.

When Edward, earl of March, at the age of nineteen, in consequence of the extraordinary turn of events, suddenly and unexpectedly in the spring of 1461, found himself recognized, at any rate by a few Yorkist lords and by many of the citizens of London, as king, the ranks of the descendants of Edward III had become somewhat depleted, but remained quite numerous, even though hopelessly divided among themselves by the tragic course of the dynastic wars of the past five or six years.

Edward IV's support from within the family was not very strong. His next eldest brother, Edmund, earl of Rutland, had lost his life at Wakefield; his younger brothers George and Richard, respectively seven and ten years younger than himself, were as yet still too young to be of much personal importance, and time would show how reliable the elder of the two would turn out to be. His eldest sister Ann had married Henry Holland, duke of Exeter, but he was a staunch Lancastrian and attainted after Northampton; she would get a divorce from him one day. His second sister Elizabeth had but recently married John de la Pole, second duke of Suffolk; his third sister Margaret was not to marry Charles the Bold, duke of Burgundy, until 1468.

The only other line from Edward III upon whom he

could count were the Bourchiers. The senior of these, his uncle by marriage, Henry, Viscount Bourchier, soon to be earl of Essex and Treasurer of England, rendered him valuable service throughout the reign, and his sons William and Humphrey (Lord Cromwell) followed suit. Henry Bourchier's brother Thomas was a most useful connexion to have in the see of Canterbury and later in the College of Cardinals.

But otherwise for the most part the descendants of Edward III remained obstinately or in some cases intermittently, Lancastrian in feeling. Henry VI and his son Edward stayed alive for another ten years, even though in fugitive condition or worse, to encourage the survival of the sentiment. Resistance to Yorkist supremacy was going to continue indefinitely from Jasper Tudor, attainted earl of Pembroke. The Beauforts and the Staffords were no lovers of the Yorkist cause, even if some of them were obliged to acquiesce or pretend to acquiesce in the turn of events. The elder Beaufort line was now represented by Margaret Beaufort, whose second husband was Henry Stafford, the second son of that Humphrey, duke of Buckingham, who had recently lost his life at Northampton. The younger line was represented by Henry II, duke of Somerset, whose reconciliation with Edward IV, so unnatural though carefully cultivated by the king, proved only temporary, and he was to lose his life for Lancaster in 1464. His two brothers were to follow his example in 1471, all without issue.

It was not, therefore, from the family of Edward III that Edward IV found the chief help that put him on the throne and kept him on it, but from the numerous and powerful relatives of his mother, Cecily Neville. Without their tremendous and sustained efforts, it is indeed a tolerable certainty that York would never have come to the throne at all. But for his marriage with the youngest of Ralph Neville's numerous progeny, Richard of York's claim to the Crown most likely would never have been advanced, or if advanced, would not have brought his son to the kingship.

From small beginnings, the Nevilles of Raby had in four generations, mainly by marriage alliances which proved highly profitable in territorial accretions and immensely fecund in off-spring, become the greatest lords in the North, greater even than their rivals, the Percys of Northumberland. The title of earl of Westmorland had been given to Ralph Neville of Raby by Richard II, even though none of his seventy and more manors was located in that shire. But Ralph married as his second wife Joan Beaufort, the daughter of John of Gaunt and Katherine Swynford, and became heavily committed to the cause of Lancaster for the rest of his life, which did not end until 1425. Nearly all his twenty-three children survived him,[1]

[1] The surviving children of Ralph Neville, earl of Westmorland were:

(a) by his first wife, Margaret, d. of Hugh Stafford, second earl of Stafford:

1. John, m. Elizabeth d. of the earl of Kent, whose eldest son and grandson by their second son became second and third earls of Westmorland.
2. Ralph m. Mary, co-heiress of Lord Ferrers.
3. Mathilda m. Peter, Lord de Mauley.
4. Philippa m. Thomas, Lord Dacre.
5. Alice m. (i) Sir Thomas Gray, and (ii) Sir Gilbert Lancaster.
6. Anne m. Sir Gilbert Umfraville of Kyme.
7. Margaret m. (i) Richard Lord Scrope, and (ii) William Cressener.

(b) by his second wife Joan Beaufort, d. of John, duke of Lancaster:

1. Richard, earl of Salisbury, m. Alice d. of Thomas, earl of Salisbury.
2. William, Lord Fauconberge and earl of Kent, m. Joan Fauconberge.
3. George, Lord Latimer, m. Elizabeth.
4. Edward, Lord Abergavenny, m. (i) Elizabeth Beauchamp, d. of Richard Beauchamp, earl of Worcester and Lord Abergavenny, and (ii) Catherine Howard, sister of John, duke of Norfolk.
5. Robert, bishop of Salisbury, later of Durham.
6. Catherine, m. (i) John Mowbray, duke of Norfolk, (ii) Thomas Strangeways, (iii) John, Viscount Beaumont, and (iv) Sir John Woodville.
7. Eleanor, m. (i) Richard, Lord Despenser, and (ii) Henry Percy, earl of Northumberland.
8. Ann, m. (i) Humphrey, duke of Buckingham, and (ii) Walter, Lord Mountjoy.
9. Joan, a nun.
10. Cecily, m. Richard, duke of York.

and most of them made important marriages which carried the Neville interest far and wide among the ranks of the peerage. It is very probable that this very influential family connexion, however, would have remained firmly behind Lancaster indefinitely, if it had not been for the marriage of the last of his offspring, Cecily, to Richard, duke of York. The couple were wedded before 1425, at a time when the Yorkist cause was no more than obscurely latent and in no sense significant. There could not, therefore, have been any *arrière pensée* in Ralph's mind when he congratulated himself on this rounding off of his children's matrimonial alliances. Nonetheless, the eventual consequences of this union went far to determine the course of English history in the second half of the century.

But even so, as it turned out, the whole of the Neville connexion was never to be aligned solidly behind York when the time came for forces to be aligned. The fact was that Ralph had begotten not one, but two families, and it was more than he could do to perpetuate a united family front. His first wife, Margaret Stafford, daughter of Hugh Stafford, second earl of Stafford (one of whose sons was destined to marry Ann Plantagenet) had borne him nine children, but as his eldest son died before him, he was succeeded in the earldom of Westmorland by his eldest grandson, Ralph II, leaving Richard, his eldest son by his marriage with Alice Montacute, sole heiress of Thomas, the somewhat impoverished earl of Salisbury, to make his own way. Furthermore, Ralph had bequeathed his Durham estates centred around Raby to his grandson and heir, but he left as jointure to Joan Beaufort the greater part of his Yorkshire lands. These important possessions were destined, therefore, not for the senior of the two families, but for the junior — a division of property and influence which was to prove a source of acrimony, dissension, and even violence between the two branches of the family. It was no mere coincidence that the second earl of Westmor-

land remained Lancastrian in sympathy — which meant
little so far as he personally was concerned, for he was an
invalid much of his life, but which meant a good deal in as
much as the senior branch and its men did not assist the
younger branch in its eventual support of York. The junior
branch itself showed reluctance at first in backing the duke
of York's claim, but it meant a very great deal when in due
course Richard, earl of Salisbury in right of his wife from
1428, rallied to the cause of the husband of his youngest
sister. To Richard of Salisbury himself, however, the cause
brought death at Pontefract after he had been captured at
Wakefield, and also to his second son Thomas, who was
killed in that battle. His mantle fell to his son Richard
Neville, already earl of Warwick in the right of his wife and
now also earl of Salisbury. To him and his connexions
more than to any other person or group of persons it was
that Richard of York's son owed his grasp and retention of
the Crown. Richard of Warwick in the process brought his
own and his family fortunes to their highest peak, brought
himself for some years to the foremost place of any subject
in the realm, only in the long run to destroy himself and
his family fortunes by his desertion of York and his
extraordinary *rapprochement* with Lancaster. The heady
wine of making and unmaking kings was too much for
him. He grossly underestimated the ability and resource of
his cousin Edward IV; his miscalculations were eventually
to cost the Neville family dear, but in 1461 such a turn of
events was unimaginable.

For several years after Towton, the problem of security
was the new government's main problem, for the cause of
Lancaster did not die easily. There was still a number of
Lancastrian lords prepared to rally to that cause, and to
raise rebellions as opportunity served. Nor is this surprising,
for not only were Henry VI and his son still at large, but
Queen Margaret, whatever her shortcomings may have

*Ann Beauchamp, countess, and
Richard Neville, earl, of Warwick*

(*The Rous Roll*, ed. Wm. Courthope (1859) pls. 56 and 57)

been, spared herself no efforts, hardships, or perils in her heroic desperation to keep her husband's, and above all her son's, cause alive by every available means. She pulled every string that she could think of, whether in Scotland, Burgundy or France (where Louis XI succeeded Charles VII in July 1461), and elsewhere, so as to embarrass Edward IV and to keep up the alarums and excursions in the Lancastrian interest.

At least she succeeded in keeping the earl of Warwick preoccupied with military affairs for several years, for to him fell the brunt of the security task. Three times he and his associates, with, or mostly without, the king, were obliged to organize and lead strong forces to the northern parts towards Scotland, to capture or re-capture border fortresses which had fallen to Scottish-Lancastrian attacks, supported by such French aid as Margaret could screw out of the wily king of France. But the time came when the springs of foreign aid dried up, and without assistance from outside the dwindling numbers and resources of active Lancastrian supporters could not hope to upset the new régime. By the early summer of 1464, all was over. The defeats at Hedgely Moor and Hexham, at which Warwick's able brother John Neville, Lord Montagu, routed the last stand of the Lancastrian survivors, marked the end of resistance. By then Margaret had shot her last bolt for the time being — it seemed then for ever. Edward IV's diplomacy had proved too much for her indefatigable but hopeless efforts. Burgundy would give her nothing but fair words and kind gifts; Louis XI agreed to a formal truce with England and to give her no further countenance; Scotland came to terms, and Henry VI himself soon had no recourse but to wander a fugitive in the north of England, no one knew where — until at last he was betrayed and captured in July 1465. Margaret and her son and a few faithful lords and followers (including ex-Chief Justice Sir John Fortescue), could do no more than retire in poverty and near-despair, to her father's castle of Koeur, at St Mihiel in Barrois.

Henry Beaufort II, duke of Somerset, the last hope for the time being of that branch of the family, together with a dozen or so other leaders had now lost their heads. It seemed unimportant that Jasper Tudor should still be at large; his as yet insignificant nephew, Henry of Richmond, had been captured with Pembroke Castle in September 1461, and his custody and marriage had been allotted to his captor, William, Lord Herbert of Raglan. Harlech Castle still held out for Lancaster, but that did not matter much either, or so it seemed. Edward IV now appeared to be secure on this throne, and the European powers recognized that fact. Pope Pius II acknowledged it; Louis

XI was anxious to obtain his goodwill and to prevent his
relations with Burgundy from becoming too cordial;
Scotland extended a truce for fifteen years; Denmark,
Castile, and Brittany had concluded treaties. York, with
the aid of the Warwick-Neville connexion, had succeeded.

It is probable that historians have fallen into the same
error as Warwick himself fell into (but in his case it
eventually cost him his life): namely the error of over-
estimating Richard Neville's abilities and under-estimating
those of Edward IV. Even so, it would no doubt be a
mistake to suppose that Edward IV deliberately set about
Warwick's ruin before his actions forced him to do so. The
train of events which eventually brought the final rupture
between the two does not bear the look of malice-afore-
thought, but sprang rather from the inevitable force of
circumstances, the consequences of which as they accumu-
lated bit by bit could not be evaded. We may indeed well
believe that Edward IV, once he felt himself firmly
established, would not be reluctant to see the support for
his throne spread more widely than it was in 1461, and to
reduce the heavy weight of Neville influence on the
government. He could scarcely have hoped to do this, in
all the circumstances, without sooner or later raising up a
new nobility, for there was nothing much to be expected
from the few and now much depleted ranks of the old. He
could count on some at least of the half-dozen new barons
he had created at his coronation, and could provide them
with lesser offices in his government, and could safely
distribute further titles to the Bourchiers and some of the
younger Nevilles. But we cannot go so far as to suppose
that he picked on a young widow to be his queen expressly
so that he might promote her father, her two sons, and her
dozen brothers and sisters, and so make the Woodvilles
rivals to the Nevilles as lions (or lionesses) under the
throne. Nonetheless, this, broadly speaking, was what
happened.

It was bad enough, from the Neville point of view, that Edward IV should have secretly married Dame Elizabeth Grey (*née* Woodville) on 1 May, 1464, and not announce the fact until 28 September. It was worse that he was obliged to make this startling revelation at a Council meeting at which Warwick and other councillors fully expected to clinch the negotiations to which Warwick had become heavily committed, and which had not been discouraged by the king, for a marriage alliance with France. What was done could not be undone, but it was very disconcerting that Edward IV should have married for no apparent reason, other than 'love', regardless of the consequences in the shape of offence and resentment on the part not only of Warwick and his associates, but also of the Yorkist lords, not to mention the chagrin felt by Louis XI, who had counted on using the alliance to keep England and Burgundy well apart.

Dame Elizabeth indeed had little to recommend her for the vacant post of Queen, from anyone's point of view, least of all from that of the Yorkist old guard, who could scarcely be expected to view with enthusiasm the elevation of a daughter and widow of hitherto staunch, even if minor, Lancastrian supporters, no matter how beautiful and attractive she might be. Even from Edward IV's point of view, her assets could hardly be counted as more than two: namely her personal charms, which must have been considerable in his eyes at least (he was himself reckoned the handsomest and most charming prince in Europe and could by then have picked and chosen for himself in any quarter); and, secondly, the large number of her male and female relatives, old and young, who could certainly now be promoted or married off to their own, and as he doubtless thought, to his own, advantage. Her father could soon become Earl Rivers and Treasurer of England, surely to the satisfaction of his wife Jacquetta of Luxembourg, who, nearly thirty years before had been the widow of the great

Queen Elizabeth Woodville
Painting at Windsor Castle. Artist unknown.

John, duke of Bedford, and had made a *mésalliance* by accepting so inferior a man as Sir Richard Woodville, and who we may be sure was not sorry to see a sudden return of grandeur and the making of the fortunes of her numerous children. Queen Elizabeth's five brothers and seven sisters, and her two sons could now be securely wedded to the king's cause.[1] As yet no open breach occurred between Edward IV and Warwick, who concealed his resentment and made a brave show of formal courtesy to the new queen, but in fact the stage was being set for a drama which would not end until it had brought tragedy not only to Earl Rivers and other Woodvilles, to Warwick himself and other Nevilles, to Henry VI and his son; utter calamity to Queen Margaret of Anjou; death to many a man; extraordinary vicissitudes to Edward IV; and finally ruin and destruction to the House of York itself. Kings who want to build securely could not afford to be 'led by blind affection and not by the rule of reason' (as Polydore Vergil was to say later on).

But although Edward IV was a man who 'would readily cast an eye upon young ladies and love them inordinately', and who made a highly imprudent marriage,[2] it would be

[1] The children of Sir Richard Woodville, Earl Rivers, and Jacquetta, dowager duchess of Bedford were:
1. Anthony, Lord Scales, later second Earl Rivers, m. (i) Lady Scales, and (ii) Mary, d. and co-heiress of Sir Henry Fitz-Lewis.
2. John, m. Catherine, dowager duchess of Norfolk.
3. Lionel, bishop of Salisbury.
4. Sir Edward, admiral.
5. Richard, later third Earl Rivers.
6. Elizabeth m. (i) Sir John Grey, Lord Ferrers of Groby, and (ii) Edward IV.
7. Margaret m. Thomas, earl of Arundel.
8. Anne, m. (i) William, Viscount Bourchier, and (ii) George Grey, earl of Kent.
9. Jacquetta, m. John, Lord Strange of Knochin.
10. Catherine, m. (i) Henry Stafford, second duke of Buckingham, and (ii) Jasper Tudor, earl of Pembroke and duke of Bedford, and (iii) Sir Richard Wingfield.
11. Mary, m. William Herbert, Lord Dunster, earl of Pembroke, later of Huntingdon.
12. Eleanor, m. Anthony, Lord Grey de Ruthin.
13. Martha, m. Sir John Bromley.

Elizabeth Woodville's children by her first marraige were Thomas Grey, later Marquis of Dorset, and Sir Richard Grey. She was to have ten children by Edward IV; all three of their sons died young and also three daughters. The surviving four daughters all lived to marry in the reign of Henry VII, the eldest of them marrying, of course, the king himself.

[2] There is no evidence that Edward IV's numerous mistresses exerted any influence on his political judgment, and very little evidence that the Queen herself did, except in what might be called 'family politics'.

an old-fashioned mistake to suppose that he therefore
neglected the tasks of government or failed to grapple with
the problems which the Lancastrian régime had left
behind it. There is no doubt that the contemporary impressions he made in the early years of his reign were
favourable, and that people expected an improvement to
occur in government. A new dynamic did indeed appear
in the workings of the administration. It is true that these
good impressions did not last very long without serious
lapse, brought about largely by the recurrence of strife and
upheavals in the course of intermittent Lancastrian risings,
and of the eventual struggle with Warwick, as well as by
general disapprobation of the Woodvilles. But the time
was to come when Edward IV would be undisputed
master in his realm, and would be deemed illustrious.

The king's principal ministers at the time of Henry VI's
last parliament in 1460 had been appointed under Yorkist
auspices, and many of these were retained when Edward
IV took over. Warwick's brother, George Neville, bishop
of Exeter, remained Chancellor until June 1467; his uncle
William, Lord Fauconberg, and soon earl of Kent,
became Steward of the Household until replaced a year or
two later by John Tiptoft, earl of Worcester — that man of
many parts, good and bad; Warwick himself filled posts of
mainly military and strategic importance, and remained
Admiral of England, Warden of the Cinque Ports, and
Captain of Calais. The Bourchiers were represented by
Henry, viscount Bourchier and soon earl of Essex, as
Treasurer, until replaced for a time by Tiptoft; and by his
younger son Humphrey, Lord Cromwell, as a Chamberlain of the Exchequer. But the rest of the ministers were
mostly lesser men, who rose to high place not so much
because of their lineage, as because of their service to the
Yorkists, combined in some instances with matrimonial
connexions with the Nevilles, as in the cases of William,
Lord Hastings, who was to hold the influential office very

close to the king, of Chamberlain of the Household, throughout the reign; John, Lord Wenlock, Chief Butler until he threw in his lot with Warwick and Lancaster later on, and — one of the councillors most in his confidence — Sir William Herbert, later earl of Pembroke.

There are many signs that Edward IV speedily revived the personal exercise of the powers of the monarch, so much fallen into abeyance under Henry VI. The absence for one reason or another of actual Council records for most of the period has obscured the revival under the king of an advisory Council, the evidence for the activity of which has been pieced together from other sources. The new Council was more of a work-a-day body of councillors, whom the king could use for advice and multifarious business as he thought fit, and whose decisions could be carried out not so much by the old cumbersome and circumlocutory methods of the privy seal office, but rather by the immediate force of the royal sign manual or signet. The signet was in the custody of the king's secretary, a confidential servant who now was usually a councillor, who began to take on the character of a public officer of importance, and who during the reign made marked progress towards the great future that lay ahead of his office.

The king himself became once again very much more the actual and less the nominal, source of administrative action. The king personally took strong measures to suppress the more flagrant outbreaks of lawlessness and violence. He personally sought to remedy the financial maladies which had beset and brought low the preceding régime. Whether he himself ever read the advice written by Sir John Fortescue, the Lancastrian ex-Chief Justice and exile, must remain problematical, but undoubtedly Edward IV's views on the importance of securing a better endowment for the Crown coincided closely with Fortescue's. The new king was in a strong position to take appropriate action. He was or became better endowed in landed estate than any of his recent predecessors. He brought to the Crown the great possessions of the duchy of York (including the inheritance of Mortimer); he confiscated the duchy of Lancaster, which he at once made into a 'corporation sole', separate and distinct from other Crown lands but annexed to the Crown in perpetuity (as it still is to-day). He was strong enough to resume 'by act of parliament' large areas of Crown lands which had been formerly alienated; he was destined also to receive numerous very large windfalls in the shape of forfeited lands from attainted rebels, whether of Lancastrians, or later of Nevilles, or later still of his attainted brother George of Clarence. Moreover, he saw to it that the management and profits of these huge territories should not be left to the tender mercies of the old Exchequer practice, with its slow and wasteful methods and load of old debts, but should remain close to his own hands. He revived the Chamber of the Household as a highly important finance office of receipt and expenditure. He had the discernment to make use of methods of management which had for long proved effective within the duchy of Lancaster, and charged particular persons with the duty of managing specific blocks of lands, making them directly responsible for the collection and payment of the profits into the Chamber. He could make a profit out of the re-coinage of 1464–5. He personally took part in mercantile ventures overseas; he kept a careful eye on the development of trade and commerce and so incidentally increased his own customs duties. His zeal for getting the royal finances on to a sound footing was greater than that of any sovereign for generations, perhaps indeed greater than any of his predecessors since King John at least. He went far to realize in practice the old medieval ideal that the 'king should live of his own', i.e. should meet the expenses of government out of his own personal and hereditary revenues, and should cut the taxation of his subjects to the bone. He could not, naturally,

H

do this all the time, for extraordinary expenses inevitably required extraordinary measures, but the fact that he attained a very considerable degree of success accounts in large part for the comparatively minor role played by parliaments in his reign.

During the first ten years of the reign, five parliaments were summoned but only three actually met. His first parliament, of 1461–2, recognized the *fait accompli* of the accession; attainted Henry VI and other Lancastrians, and confiscated the duchy of Lancaster (the shade of Richard II must have smiled wryly); confirmed the judicial acts of the Lancastrian kings; and passed some minor legislation; but no money grant was asked for or given. Another parliament was summoned for 1463, only to be abandoned because of irregularities in the county elections. But another was summoned and lasted with five prorogations until 1465. In its first session it granted an aid on somewhat novel lines (later the novelties were dropped) for 'the hastey defence of the realm', i.e. against Lancastrian risings; in its second session it followed precedent by granting tunnage and poundage and the subsidy on wool to the king for life, and passed a number of statutes mainly of commercial interest. The parliament of 1467–8 saw two short sessions and three prorogations. In the first of these the king made a notable announcement that he intended 'to live of his own and to spare the Commons', a very welcome statement no doubt, and which anyway precluded him from asking for any more money on that occasion; but another substantial Act of Resumption carried further his policy of recovering alienated Crown lands. A parliament was summoned for 1469 but never met, for the king by then was preoccupied with more pressing matters. The next one that met was in 1470–1, which, as it turned out, was not in the name of Edward IV, but in that of Henry VI. Some very curious events had occurred in the meantime.

Among the many circumstances that brought about the defection of the earl of Warwick and the Neville-Lancastrian *coup d'état* of 1470, an important place must be given to irreconcilable divergence of opinion in the sphere of foreign affairs. It seems probable that Warwick accepted with as good a grace as he could Edward IV's marriage with Elizabeth Woodville, even though this had meant the reduction to farce of his attempts at negotiating a matrimonial alliance with the royal House of France; probable also that he was prepared to stomach for a time at least the spectacle of Woodville family promotion and aggrandizement. But when the time came for Edward IV's intentions regarding Burgundy to be revealed, which involved a complete reversal of Warwick's own ideas on the subject, it was the beginning of the end from Warwick's standpoint. He had probably committed himself too far to a course of friendship with France and of hostility towards Burgundy to be able to re-adjust himself. Soon overt treason beckoned him on.

It is clear that Edward IV, as part of his many-sided activity, gave very careful attention to foreign affairs, and employed many diplomatic agents. It looks very much as though from the start he was determined to make diplomatic headway in Europe, which indeed he greatly needed to do. Although he doubtless had to allow Warwick to appear to take a large share in these matters, he seems to have had no intention of allowing him to dominate the real course of diplomacy or to dictate the more conclusive negotiations. The vital decisions were taken behind his back or in spite of him. Broadly speaking it was Edward IV's (and the Woodvilles') policy to pursue close alliance with Burgundy, whilst it remained Warwick's (and the Nevilles') to pursue alliance with France at the expense of Burgundy. Thus Edward IV came to private terms with Charles of Charolais in October 1466, and in May 1467 he received at court Charles's natural brother, Anthony (the

Bastard of Burgundy), ostensibly to promote a feat of arms between him and Edward IV's brother-in-law, Anthony Woodville, Lord Scales, but actually to discuss privately a matrimonial alliance between Edward's sister Margaret and the heir of Burgundy — all at a time when Warwick was being lavishly entertained and flattered by Louis XI.

Warwick's indignation on his return to England to find that the ground had been cut from beneath his feet, and on witnessing the king's extremely cavalier treatment of the French envoys whom he had brought back with him, was more than he could conceal. But the Nevilles were now riding for a fall. On 8 June, Edward IV personally and suddenly relieved George Neville of the Great Seal, and it was no consolation that George had so recently been promoted to the archbishopric of York. The announcement soon followed of the betrothal of Margaret to Charles, by then duke of Burgundy. Warwick retired in dudgeon to his northern castle of Middleham, and refused to come to court even under safe-conduct. Unable, however, to deflect Edward IV from his purpose or to secure the dismissal of the Woodvilles, of Herbert or of any others from the king's counsels, he managed to come to a nominal reconciliation in January 1468.

He could not prevent the furtherance of Edward IV's diplomatic policies. An important treaty for promoting commercial intercourse with Flanders and Brabant was soon ratified; the marriage contract between Duke Charles and Margaret was signed in February; and a defensive alliance against all other powers followed, together with a similar agreement with Francis II, duke of Brittany. The tide was running fast against Louis XI, and also against his friend the earl of Warwick. Hostilities against France in alliance with Burgundy and Brittany became imminent, and the parliament of 1468 made money grants mainly with that warlike purpose in view.

The appearance of a split in the Yorkist ranks naturally

proved encouraging to Lancastrians everywhere. Plots re-appeared, and so did Jasper Tudor, who made an incursion into Wales and managed to capture Denbigh, but was obliged thereafter to withdraw, whereupon Harlech Castle at long last surrendered to Lord Herbert, who was rewarded with Jasper's already forfeited earldom of Pembroke.

But in the meantime Warwick was making his own plot. He had some time previously aimed at seducing to his side no less a person than the heir-presumptive to the throne, Edward IV's brother, George, duke of Clarence, and had sought to promote a marriage between him and his own elder daughter Isabel. Any such project had been peremptorily forbidden by the king, but now the time had come for Warwick to achieve what he doubtless regarded as a master-stroke. In April 1469, he had no difficulty, as Captain of the place, in slipping over to Calais, where in July he was quietly joined by his brother the archbishop of York, and by Clarence. There the prelate obliged by joining Isabel and Clarence in holy matrimony on 11 July. Papal dispensation had already been obtained for the marriage of these second cousins. All was in order, and there was nothing that Edward IV could do about it.

Worse was to follow. Warwick and Clarence lost no time in returning to England and making a declaration against the existing government. A Neville rising, carefully organized and timed, broke out in the north under the banner of one 'Robin Redesdale', and a march south began. The defeat of one section of the insurgents by Warwick's brother John, Lord Montague (who had recently been given the Percy estates and title of earl of Northumberland, and consequently did not like the demand made by this section for the restoration of the Percies) failed to prevent a rapid Yorkist *débâcle*. The fact was that Edward IV had been taken by surprise and was left defenceless when the forces rallying to his support led by William Herbert, earl of Pembroke, and Humphrey Stafford, the new earl of Devon, were shattered at Edgecote on 26 July, 1469. The result of this bloody encounter was that at Warwick's instigation, the king's father-in-law Earl Rivers, the earl of Pembroke and his brother Richard, and the earl of Devon, all lost their heads, whilst Edward IV himself was politely but firmly detained by Archbishop Neville and Warwick, and escorted first to Warwick Castle and then to Middleham. It seemed as though York was now safely secured in the pocket of Neville, but in fact Warwick had over-reached himself.

The public in general did not view with any favour the turn of events; they could not tolerate a situation in which one former king languished in the Tower, and their present king became a puppet at Middleham. Any idea that Warwick may have entertained of making Clarence king instead of Edward was doomed to failure. Warwick, although personally popular and widely admired for his achievements in the past ten years, found that he could not carry on the government with the king under restraint, and was simply obliged to let Edward IV do as he wished and to return to London as he pleased. Warwick could do no more than accept the position for the moment, and Edward IV, with remarkable statesmanship and self-restraint, pretended that nothing untoward had happened. Outwardly he remained friendly towards the Nevilles, and even consented to a betrothal of his eldest daughter, Elizabeth, to Warwick's nephew, George, the son of John Neville, earl of Northumberland, and elevated the boy to the dukedom of Bedford in anticipation of a future alliance, which, however, was never to take place.[1]

But Warwick was not to be won over; his disgruntled ambitions would not allow him to accept the *status quo*, and Clarence was still willing to aid and abet him. How far

[1] It was George's fate to be deprived of the dukedom and peerage in 1478 on the grounds that he had not sufficient livelihood to support it.

they were personally concerned in a fresh disturbance which soon broke out in Lincolnshire remains uncertain, but there is no doubt that they were prepared to profit from it if possible. In any case Edward IV soon regarded them as implicated, and doubtless determined that the time had come for settling the score. He suppressed the disturbance quickly and ruthlessly, and peremptorily summoned Warwick and Clarence to his presence. But they would not come, and instead took to flight and sought refuge in Calais. But the king had anticipated this move, and had taken steps to prevent their admission on any account.[1] In the circumstances, there was nothing that they could do but to enter France (5 May, 1470), and see what scheme they might be able to contrive there, with the assistance of Louis XI's ever-ready cunning.

A scheme was indeed contrived, and one of the most remarkable in English history. It involved no less a *volte-face* than Warwick's abandoning the cause of York altogether and agreeing to transfer his whole support to Lancaster. It required all of Louis XI's skill and patience to persuade Margaret of Anjou to meet and speak to the detested architect of her misfortunes, but, after Warwick had been kept on his suppliant knees before her for a sufficient time, in the end she came to terms with him. He was to restore Henry VI; his second daughter Ann was to marry her son Prince Edward; her faithful friends and fellow-exiles were to be restored to their possessions and places; he was to govern as lieutenant until Prince Edward came of age or succeeded his father. Louis XI was delighted and promised all suitable aid to carry the scheme into effect. The difficulty, however, in all this was to find any

---

[1] Whilst waiting on shipboard off Calais, Warwick's daughter Isabel gave birth to a son, who died young. It was the daughter of Isabel and Clarence, Margaret, born 1473, who was destined to become the countess of Salisbury and because of her descent, was beheaded by Henry VIII in 1541. Their surviving son, Edward, earl of Warwick, born 1476, suffered a like fate at Henry VII's hands in 1499. See p. 160.

way of satisfying Clarence. The best they could think of
for him was to promise that should by any chance Prince
Edward fail to have heirs, then the reversion of the Crown
should go to him and his heirs.

A poor sop it was for Clarence, who in consequence
would, as soon as it was safe, think up a line of action of his
own, and re-discover the advantages (for a time) of being
a king's brother. Indeed Edward IV's agents were soon at
work upon him, secretly encouraging him to that end.

But Warwick's scheme succeeded, and without a battle.
Edward IV was not fully prepared for the rapid turn of
events, and when Warwick and his allies landed in Devon-
shire on 13 September, he was still in the north where he
had personally coped with a small but carefully timed
rising. He was on the way south to meet the invaders when
unexpected treachery on the part of Warwick's brother
John Neville (who had been deprived of the earldom of
Northumberland after the affair of the previous year, and
had been fobbed off with a marquisate without territorial
endowment) compelled him, in dramatic circumstances
and by a hair's breadth, to escape capture by instant flight
and setting sail from Lynn to Holland. He was accom-
panied only by his faithful young brother Richard of
Gloucester, his brother-in-law the second Earl Rivers, by
Lord Hastings, ever-devoted to Edward IV even though
he was Warwick's brother-in-law, by Lord Say and Sele,
and very few other followers. On the same day, 3 October,
Henry VI found himself once again occupying the royal
apartments in the Tower. It seemed as though all was over
with the House of York.

III

York Triumphant

FROM every point of view, Edward IV's complete recovery of his realm within eight months of his flight was a masterly performance. In the process his striking abilities were revealed as never before nor after; his tremendous resilience, energy, and courage; his brilliant military capacity, combined with a good measure of guile and cunning, brought him quickly to victory over all his opponents, Neville and Lancastrian, and also brought his realm to a state of tranquillity and stability for the rest of his life such as it had not known for many decades.

His policy in marrying his sister Margaret to the duke of Burgundy brought abundant fruit; indeed but for that he might well have been unable to make his recovery. For it was with Burgundian aid that he managed to fit out a small expedition in early March, 1471, and land once again in England. It is one of the little ironies of history that he found it highly convenient to model himself at first on the example set by Henry Bolingbroke in 1399. After a difficult passage and probings on the Norfolk coast, he finally landed where Bolingbroke had landed, at Ravenspur (was it not still Lancastrian property, and had not Edward annexed the duchy ten years ago?). Once landed, he found it expedient to give out, as Bolingbroke had given out, that he had only come to claim his duchy — the duchy of York this time. For the populace showed no great enthusiasm as yet for helping him back on to the throne. The popularity he had enjoyed earlier on seems to have evaporated a good deal, and in any event Warwick's preparations

Edward IV

Painting at Windsor Castle. Artist unknown.

to cope with any incursion seemed to be too efficient to be lightly evaded. The situation Edward found was far from encouraging, and he took his life in his hands as, with small forces which did not materially increase for some time, he pushed southwards to seek ways and means of bringing the issue to a decision. But as it turned out, Warwick's plans for halting Edward on his march south failed. No one intervened. The lack of intervention was due in part at least to the unwillingness either of Henry Percy, who had earlier been restored by Edward to the earldom of Northumberland, or of John Neville, Marquis Montagu, whose enjoyment of the earldom had consequently been cut short, to show his hand. Together they could easily have terminated Edward's career; either could have decisively intervened. But Percy would not move, though his family had been traditionally Lancastrian, and lesser northern lords therefore would not move either. Montagu was in the field, but shut himself up at Pontefract, letting Edward march round him to reach Doncaster and Nottingham. He threatened to attack Lancastrian forces at Newark, but they promptly retired. Warwick himself withdrew into Coventry and would not budge nor accept Edward's challenges. It may be that Warwick deliberately awaited Clarence's arrival with reinforcements, possibly at Clarence's behest. But Edward knew by then that brother Clarence was on the way to join himself with substantial forces raised in the name of Henry VI. Clarence was about to perjure himself once again, and to re-discover his loyalty to his own family. A touching scene of reconciliation occurred, and after some efforts were made to induce Warwick to submit, the three Yorkist brothers, Edward, George, and Richard left him at Coventry to contemplate the turn of events whilst they pressed on to London. Edward had already re-proclaimed himself king, and the earl of Warwick was now honoured with the official designation of 'his great rebel'. By 11 April Edward IV entered London unopposed; Archbishop Neville's hasty attempts to bolster up resistance by parading the bewildered Henry VI through the streets proved to be futile, and he himself lost no time in humbly submitting himself to the once-again rising sun of York. So Edward IV was enabled to hasten without impediment to the sanctuary of Westminster and to receive a goodly gift from his queen, who had been in refuge there ever since her husband had been away, and there, in early November, 1470 had given birth to their fourth child, but first-born son. At that moment of exaltation, it must have seemed to them that marriage for mere love had its compensations.

Archbishop Bourchier, now also Cardinal, at once obliged with a token re-coronation of Edward, and Cecily, dowager duchess of York, could joyfully receive her restored royal son and her first grandson at the family town-residence of Baynards Castle. The 're-adeption' (or restoration) of Henry VI was over — except for the fighting.

Within a few weeks the fighting was also over, and the Houses of Neville and Lancaster irretrievably ruined. It was on 14 April that Edward IV out-manœuvred, out-generalled, and out-fought his 'great rebel' and the forces he had brought down from Coventry as far as Barnet. By the time that short fierce battle was over, Warwick was dead, slain in attempting to flee at the end, and his brother Montagu was no more. But John de Vere, earl of Oxford, escaped, and lived on to fight again (and with more success) fourteen years later. On the other side two Bourchiers and the faithful Lord Say and Sele paid their forfeit for York. Henry VI himself, brought to the field by Edward IV, had witnessed his last battle, and was on the way back to the Tower, but this time with an unwonted fellow-traveller — the surviving Neville brother, George, archbishop of York.[1]

[1] George Neville was subsequently released, but later on he was suspected of correspondence with Lancastrian survivors, and on 25 April, 1472 he

On the same day as the battle of Barnet was won and lost, Margaret of Anjou, Prince Edward and his wife Ann Neville, and other exiles, at long last landed in England, at Weymouth. She had delayed her departure from exile too long; partly perhaps because of her distrust of Warwick, of her disbelief in the permanence of his success and intentions, and of her reluctance to commit the precious heir of Lancaster to the hazards of the restoration; and when at length she did set out, adverse winds postponed her sailing. The news of the disaster at Barnet was a crushing blow to her hopes, and she was probably right in her instinctive wish to return with her son to France at once. But the counsel of such Lancastrian lords as rallied to her, the surviving Beauforts, the Courtneys of Devon, and others, and the prospect of being able to join forces with Jasper Tudor and his Welshmen from North Wales and the Marches, together prevailed. The decision was taken, after a feint-move towards London, to march up the Severn valley to affect a junction with Jasper and to try the verdict of another battle. It was a fatal decision; the great skill of Edward IV's scouts in ascertaining the moves of the Lancastrian forces; his master-stroke in causing them to be denied refuge in Gloucester, and the extreme rapidity of his marches, resulted, not in their juncture with Jasper, but in their collision with him in full array at Tewkesbury on 4 May. The last hopes of Lancaster lay stricken when that field had been fought; the heir himself, Prince Edward, was slain fleeing from the field. Edmund Beaufort II, duke of Somerset and his brother John, Courtney, and more than a dozen other Lancastrian leaders had fought their last battle, for they were killed then and there or lost their heads within a day or two. Margaret of Anjou also had fought her last fight and was reduced to the ultimate

returned to the Tower and he was sent over to confinement at either Hammes or Guisnes. He was released in 1475 and allowed to return, but he died 8 June, 1476.

humiliation of capture and submission.[1] Her so recently-acquired daughter-in-law,[2] Ann Neville, bereft of her father 'the great rebel', and of her husband, and no longer even titular princess of Wales, now had no visible prospects as merely the impecunious sister-in-law of rapacious George, duke of Clarence, whose treachery had done so much to destroy her precarious hopes. The fantastic tricks which destiny still had in store for her were as yet hidden.

Some flickers of Lancastrian resistance lingered on. An alarm in the north was quickly suppressed by Henry Percy, who now hastened to show his hand on Edward IV's side. A far more serious threat came from Thomas Neville, the 'Bastard of Fauconberg',[3] who concocted an audacious plan for capturing London, and came within sight of success. But that *coup* did not in fact come off, and after a few days' fighting and uncertainty, the attempt petered out. On 21 May Edward IV was able to enter London in triumph, with Margaret of Anjou perforce in his train. The same night, her husband, Henry VI, left the Tower of London for the last time, and for ever. Maybe he died a natural death; maybe Yorkist 'reason of state' pricked him on to a peace which he had never known in life, except perhaps within his own soul.

Jasper Tudor had not been in time to appear at Tewkesbury, but he was still able to save the ultimate future. He retired to Chepstow and then to Pembroke Castle, to sail from Tenby to France, taking with him out of Pembroke Castle his nephew Henry, called earl of Richmond. But

---

[1] Her unhappy fate was to remain in Edward IV's hands until under the terms of the Treaty of Picquigny of 1476 she was released for cash and allowed to return to France. Louis XI gave her a small pension but only on condition that she surrendered to him all rights of succession she might have to any lands in France. She lived on, in extreme poverty and neglect, in Anjou until 1482. Long enough indeed, but not quite long enough to enable her to hear of the ruin of her enemies, except Clarence.

[2] It is quite clear that Prince Edward and Ann Neville were in fact married at Amboise on 13 December, 1470.

[3] Thomas was a natural son of William Neville, Lord Fauconberg, earl of Kent, an uncle of the earl of Warwick.

adverse winds forced them to land in Brittany, where duke
Francis II, more reliable perhaps as a host than Louis XI,
gave them refuge. That was a pity from Edward IV's point
of view, but only a very slight spot on his fully risen and
flaming sun. York had at last triumphed over all.

Edward IV had now attained a position of strength such
as no king of England had secured for more than a hundred
years, perhaps indeed not since the days of Edward I in
his zenith. For the remaining twelve years of his life and
reign he was without rival; he was undisputed master of
his realm, and he was not, as it turned out, to be drawn
into a renewal of the French war, despite appearances to
the contrary at one stage. He was to show himself a realist
who sought after solid gains rather than vainglory. He did
much to consolidate the monarchy, to rehabilitate its
finances, and to restore its prestige. He stopped the process
of decay in monarchy and government which had been
both cause and effect of the civil wars of the preceding
half-century; he went far to remedy 'the lack of politique
reule' and governance which had brought Henry VI to
disaster; he was not to be led astray by Henry V's martial
dreams; he grasped firmly the financial nettles which
Henry IV had either evaded or sown. He achieved much
that Richard II had tried but failed to do. The two great
duchies of Lancaster and of York were now firmly vested
in the Crown, and there was no great magnate left to
overshadow the king. A period of stability and progress
seemed assured; commerce revived; merchant adventure,
encouraged and participated in by the king himself,
flourished; prosperity re-appeared; law and order were
better observed; the first fruits of humanism ripened at
court, in noble households, and in other high places;
Caxton could begin his epoch-making work in England
under the patronage of such diverse personalities as the
king himself, his brother-in-law Anthony Woodville,

*Anthony Woodville, Lord Scales, second
Earl Rivers, presents a copy of his book
'Sayings of the Philosphers' to Edward IV,
Queen Elizabeth, and Prince Edward,
afterwards Edward V*

(Lambeth Palace Library, MS. 265, fo. iv)

second earl Rivers, and John Tiptoft, earl of Worcester,
who saw nothing incompatible in combining 'butchery'
with highly cultivated literary tastes (indeed it is to be
feared that his reading gave him fresh ideas for his more
blood-thirsty pursuits). By these and many other activities
in court circles, England was given a more 'modern' tone
— in the contemporary sense — and brought into line
with European trends. But a dozen years were not enough
to bring rehabilitation to full fruition. The king was to die

before he was forty-one years of age; a certain lassitude and lack of purpose was to settle upon him, and before the end came, he was, in an excess of exasperation and power, to resort to legal fratricide, and so to present the spectacle of York divided against itself — a spectacle which might attain more monstrous proportions once he was dead. Furthermore, the long years of diplomatic success which he had enjoyed for most of his reign were to be turned into disappointment and failure, and to give way to open hostilities before the end came.

When Edward IV resumed the kingship in 1471, he no longer had to find places for any of the Neville family. The Chancellorship was freely at his disposal, and short tenures of it by Richard Stillington, bishop of Bath and Wells, and by Laurence Booth, bishop of Durham, gave way in May 1474 to the appointment of Thomas Rotheram, bishop of Lincoln and later archbishop of York, who remained in the office until the end. The only descendant of Edward III who found a place among the principal ministers was Henry Bourchier, earl of Essex, who was to stay as Treasurer for the rest of his nephew's reign; the ever-faithful Lord Hastings likewise remained Chamberlain of the Household and replaced Warwick as Captain of Calais for the rest of Edward IV's life (and his own). Thomas, Lord Stanley (who before October, 1473, was to do very well for himself as the third[1] husband of Margaret Beaufort, countess of Richmond, and therefore as the step-father of a certain exile in Brittany) was to be Steward of the Household for the rest of the Yorkist régime. The first Earl Rivers had indeed fallen by the wayside, but his son and heir Anthony Woodville, the ablest and most highly cultivated of his family, found a place at court and kept it until the

---

[1] Strictly speaking he was her fourth husband, as she was married in infancy to John de la Pole, duke of Suffolk. This marriage was presumably dissolved early and was no more than nominal, though legal. Her marriage to Edmund Tudor ensued; she married before 1464, Henry Stafford, second son of the first duke of Buckingham, who died in October 1471.

I

end. The king's younger brother, Richard, duke of
Gloucester, who had fully shared in all his king's adventures, figured now as Admiral of England and throve in
his brother's trust. John Russell, soon to be bishop of
Lincoln, took over the Privy Seal from Rotheram in 1474
and held it until the end of the reign. Very slight changes
occurred among the lesser offices, and a remarkable —
probably unprecedented — degree of continuity of office
was preserved. It seems as though Edward IV had now got
together a team of officers that suited him and upon whom
he was prepared to rely. Apart from the trouble which was
still to arise with Clarence, there is little sign of friction
among Edward IV, his relatives, his ministers and his
councillors in these years. He himself was now indisputably
head of the government, and no one ventured to question
his appointments.

He soon showed himself determined to consolidate
further the finances of the Crown. Additional accessions of
forfeited estates from the Nevilles and Lancastrians swelled
the total of his landed property, and there were to be yet
additional gains when Clarence was no more. He could
now carry further the experiments in estate management
which he had initiated in the first half of his reign, and
could ensure the payment of very substantial receipts
direct to the Chamber, and so keep them close to his own
control. He could tackle seriously the whole question of
retrenchment and economy in his own household (always
the bottomless well of Lancastrian finance), and by his far-
reaching Household Ordinance of 1478 he went far to
regulate domestic arrangements so as to keep expenditure
in bounds whilst preserving the outward show of royal
magnificence, the importance of which he fully understood
but for which Henry VI, in his humble other-worldliness,
had neither zest nor money. By this measure he set the
household on the main lines it was to follow for generations.
His financial credit naturally revived with the revival of

fortune, and he could borrow freely once more from foreign and home lenders, especially the mercantile classes who from the start had largely replaced the gentry as the financial backers of the Yorkists. He was also to find other ways and means of improving his resources before his reign was over. He succeeded in making the Crown not only solvent, but affluent.

There were to be only three more parliaments in his time. The first of these was to exist for a longer period than any previous parliament, spread as it was over seven short sessions, lasting in all from October 1472 to March 1475. It made some grants in aid of the projected French expedition, dealt with a number of attainders or reversals of attainders, and passed a few pieces of miscellaneous and minor legislation. The second parliament sat for about five weeks in early 1478 but did little apart from giving the king authority to dispose of Clarence. No further parliament was summoned at all until very near the end of the reign, in January 1483. For five, not entirely peaceful, years, Edward IV was able to do without a representative parliament — a longer interval between parliaments than had occurred since the days of Edward I. But if he could do without taxation he could readily do without parliaments, and so 'spare the poor Commons'. That was precisely what the Commons liked, and there were not as yet any Whigs born before their time to tell them that they ought to have known better.

For advice Edward IV had, of course, his councillors, and could from time to time seek the counsel of the lords spiritual and temporal in great council assembled, and there were to be no complaints that he was a king who ruled without due and proper consultations. He in fact went far to restore what had been the normal balance between the monarchy and the other institutions which had prevailed in the old days before civil strife and antagonisms had upset it.

The time came, however, when extraordinary charges, especially those arising from war with the Scots, obliged him to summon another, and as it happened, his last, parliament. In January 1483, a parliament met and made him a grant for these purposes.

Neither ministers, councillors, magnates, nor parliaments gave Edward IV much difficulty in these years. Nor did the bishops. The circumstances of his accession and restoration enabled him to obtain a much stronger hold over the episcopate than had ever been possible under the Lancastrian governments, especially that of Henry VI. The occurrence of no fewer than twenty vacancies during the last twelve years of his reign made it easy for him to reconstruct the bench of bishops. The papacy proved acquiescent, and now it was the king's influence, not, as it often had been, that of magnate families, which determined the choice of episcopal recruits. His choice fell frequently upon men whose earlier careers had been spent in the service of the Crown, whose bent was legalistic and administrative rather than theological or pietistic. In this sphere as in others, the Crown now asserted its influence, and pointed the way for further predominance in the future. A subservient episcopate was no invention of the Tudors.

It was not likely that Edward IV would be prepared to overlook the machinations of Louis XI which had brought such a *débâcle* in 1470, the consequences of which he had now so triumphantly overcome with a modicum of assistance from Burgundian territories. His resentment at the treatment he had received at once brought into prospect a serious war of retaliation with France.

In the first session of the first parliament of his restoration, Edward IV announced his intention of going to war against his ancient and mortal adversary the king of France, and talked very big about his old inheritance of the Crown and realm of France, of Normandy, Gascony, and Guienne. It sounded as if Henry V were come again, and the Commons as usual rallied to the call. Without hesitation they voted a large supply of archers, but granted in cash only a special income tax of one-tenth of landed revenues for one year, and on condition that the money was to be held safely until the prospective army was in train, and subject to refund if the expedition had not set out by Michaelmas, 1474. The insufficiency of this contribution was recognized in the second session, and a further modest grant made, subject to similar conditions. But defects in the collection of what had been granted obliged amendments to be made by the time of the sixth session of the same parliament, an additional subsidy was made, and the time-limit was extended for a year.

The Commons begrudged parting with their money. What they had granted seemed to their generation a lot, and indeed was more than had been voted in all the previous years of the reign put together. But Edward IV was clearly determined to 'cash in' on the policy of war-like moves against France to the maximum extent possible, whilst it still remained a practicable policy. It was about this time that he resorted especially to the device of extorting 'benevolences', i.e. 'free-will offerings' from a variety of his subjects, few of whom were in a position to refuse to contribute when asked. The ladies concerned could scarcely refuse (even if they wanted to) a kingly kiss; and the men could still less venture to ignore a writ of Privy Seal. The seventh and last session of the parliament followed up with a further grant. Treaties of alliance with Charles, duke of Burgundy, were sealed, and at long last, towards the end of June 1475, Edward IV set out for France with probably the largest and best equipped army that had ever made the crossing, and supported by a fine array of martial Yorkist magnates.

But Edward IV was not in fact a Henry V born again, and it is very doubtful whether he ever seriously thought of

himself in such a role. By mid-August the enterprise was
over, and without any battle at all. For one thing, Charles
of Burgundy proved to be a broken reed, and when it came
to the point, had little help to offer other than verbal; for
another thing, Louis XI had no mind at all to try the
consequences of another Agincourt, and lost no time in
offering handsome terms, not indeed in land (the last thing
he would ever part with) but in hard cash, to induce
Edward IV to withdraw from France. A French Crown
was not to be had, but 75,000 crowns of gold cash down
and 50,000 more per annum for life were quite enough to
make Edward IV willing to abandon his war-like display,
to wash his hands of the infuriated Charles of Burgundy,
and to retire — a decision facilitated in council by Louis
XI's discreet but liberal distribution of *douceurs* among
Edward's principal advisers. The Bridge of Picquigny saw
a personal meeting and exchange of pleasantries (under
heavy security arrangements) between the two kings. The
Treaty settled at that town shelved all awkward questions
about claims and territories by referring them to future
arbitration, fixed the terms, established a truce for seven
years, and concluded a contract of marriage between the
Dauphin and Edward's eldest daughter Elizabeth, to be
fulfilled when they became of suitable age. Another 50,000
crowns were acceptable enough to Edward IV as the price
of the release of Margaret of Anjou, for whom he could
have had no possible use any longer.

The 75,000 crowns were duly paid over, and Edward IV
set out homewards, and by September 28 was back in
London, without glory, but with commonsense on his side.
Burgundy declared himself betrayed, but forgot to mention
that his contribution had been negligible; many war-like
spirits did not like the outcome. In fact Edward IV, on
behalf of himself and his successors, had renounced the
pretentious legacy of Edward III and Henry V, had
abandoned in practice though not in theory the hollow

claims of the English monarchy to the realm of France; had put an end to useless bloodshed and devastation; had prevented the Hundred Years' War from extending into another century. At the same time, he had carried appreciably further the principal aim of his domestic policy — the better endowment of the Crown. It was realism with a vengeance, even if Nicolo Machiavelli was as yet only six years of age.

It was indeed unfortunate for Charles the Bold (or Rash as the French called him), but within eighteen months his impetuosity in another and different quarrel brought his career to a sudden and violent end before the walls of Nancy, in January 1477. He left as the sole heiress of his great domains his daughter Mary by his first wife. She was still unmarried and was free to choose her husband as she wished. So great a matrimonial prize was more than enough to flutter the dovecots in all the courts of Europe. To the court of Edward IV it brought in its train crisis and tragedy. For its repercussions evoked a conclusion to the smouldering feud between the king and his brother George, duke of Clarence.

Clarence had for many years postured in the role of black sheep in the Yorkist family. Why his course of conduct should have followed the lines it did it is difficult to conjecture in the absence of much contemporary evidence of his character other than that afforded by his actions. That he had developed into a vain and conceited fellow, incapable of loyalty to anything outside of himself and devoid of stability of purpose, seems only too clear. He had at an early age come under the spell of the earl of Warwick, under whose tutelage he had been in part brought up, and to Warwick must fall the blame for having first seduced him from proper loyalty to his brother the king by his proposition that he should marry his daughter Isabel, and so ally himself closely with the Neville in-

terest. Warwick also did not scruple to exploit Clarence's
position as heir-presumptive until 1470–1. Inflated ideas of
self-importance brought him into open conflict with his
brother the king in 1469 and again in 1470. He thus
exposed himself to the perils and penalties of treason, but
soon threw over Warwick when he saw that he was not
going to get much gratification for himself out of a
Lancastrian restoration, except the hollow one of being
designated reversionary heir in the then improbable event
of a failure of Lancastrian male heirs. The fact that his
wife's sister was now married to the Lancastrian prince
could not have been viewed by him with any enthusiasm.
He therefore deserted Warwick and Lancaster as soon as it
became safe for him to do so, and no doubt he expected for
his pains marks of favour and esteem from his brother,
which were not forthcoming.

He certainly thought for one thing that when the battles
were over, and Ann Neville was so promptly widowed, he
would at least be able to secure the whole of the Warwick
inheritance in the right of his wife. But he failed to reckon
that his younger brother Richard of Gloucester (then
nineteen years of age) knew a desirable co-heiress when he
saw one. Richard determined to marry Ann himself — he
had known her since boyhood — and, despite considerable
efforts on Clarence's part to prevent it, marry her he did;
nor could Clarence prevent his brother the king from
insisting upon a more or less normal partition of the
Warwick lands between the two of them when the time
came. Nor was Clarence pleased not to receive the favour
of exemption from some of the provisions of the Resumption
Act of 1473. Moreover, he soon saw that it was not he, but
Richard, who rose steadily in the king's confidence and trust.

As it happened, Clarence's wife Isabel died in December,
1476, and no sooner was Charles the Bold dead, than
Clarence saw himself as a splendid match for the heiress of
Burgundy, a vision in which his own sister Margaret, the

Isobel Neville, duchess, and George, duke, of Clarence

(*The Rous Roll, loc. cit.*, pls. 62 and 63)

dowager duchess of Burgundy, dotingly but foolishly encouraged him. But Edward IV naturally would have none of such a scheme for the vast aggrandizement of his totally unreliable brother George, and would not even countenance his own queen's idea that her brother Anthony Woodville, Earl Rivers, also recently widowered, might fit the bill instead. Edward, ever realistic in these matters, had no desire to see Burgundy added to the family possessions. To him it was a relief when Mary of Burgundy soon married Maximilian of Austria and so removed tempting opportunities from his family's range of aspiration.

But Clarence's injured pride and the renewed exasperation which he gave to his brother brought them both to extreme courses. Scandalous exhibitions of spite and spleen by Clarence, and a not much better performance by

Edward in retaliation, followed by impudent defiance on Clarence's part, brought him to the Tower under arrest, and by 18 February, 1478, his life was at an end. He was attainted in the parliament of January 1478, found guilty of high treason, and sentenced to forfeiture and death. Edward IV alone was responsible for what happened. The charges against Clarence were carefully formulated, and it is hard to say that they were not substantially a true bill. Many a man had lost his head for less than Clarence's offences. But the king alone accused him, and no one spoke for him in public. Even so, Edward IV might well have taught his brother a severe lesson, and stopped short of fratricide. But he did not; he was too powerful now for any one to restrain him; he could not even restrain himself. He was to regret his action in his own life-time. He forgot that, although 'stone dead hath no fellow', there had once been four Yorkist brothers, then three, and now there were to be only two. The precedent of slaughter within the Yorkist family had been set, and its consequences might be far-reaching.

It is probable that Edward IV's handling of the Clarence episode was a symptom of a decline in his powers of judgment. It may be that adversity rather than success brought out his best qualities, and that the position of untrammelled power to which he had attained blurred the sense of caution and policy which had in the past been his. The very success which he had obtained and the fulfilment of so many of his projects seem to have left him with no clear objectives. Very likely his tendency to over-indulgence in sensual pleasures of one kind or another induced a loss of grip on matters of state. At any rate, during what were to prove to be his last few years, his good fortune deserted him, especially in the sphere of foreign affairs, and he was to feel the sharp pangs of disillusionment and failure in some of his most cherished schemes before the end came.

His hopes of maintaining the *status quo* in Western

Europe by cementing a marriage alliance between the son of the new duke and duchess of Burgundy and one of his own daughters, which came to be actively negotiated, were not fulfilled. Worse still, the marriage between his eldest daughter and the dauphin of France, supposed to have been assured by the Treaty of Picquigny, never took place. Instead all his hopes were dashed by Louis XI's triumph in securing a match between the dauphin and the daughter of Maximilian and Mary of Burgundy. Louis XI had got the better of him, and now it was England that was isolated, and in the circumstances the king of France saw no reason to continue the pension with which he had been buying off the intervention of the king of England. For England without Burgundy was not much of a menace to France, and Edward IV would have to think again and act again if he wanted to carry any weight on the Continent.

The only satisfactory turn of events for Edward IV in these years was the very capable manner in which his brother Richard of Gloucester dealt with a fresh outbreak of trouble on the Scots border. Edward IV had not refrained since 1471 from trying to make capital out of divisions and plots at the court of James III, and after a period of uneasy and shifty transactions, a project was formed of seeking to recover Berwick, which had remained in Scots hands ever since the events of 1461. Richard was given command of this enterprise, and in the course of it acquitted himself with distinction. Scotland itself was invaded more than once; Berwick was recaptured and held, and much public praise was earned by Richard. For two years Edward IV managed to keep a large army moving on the Borders and in Scotland without summoning a parliament to give aid. To be able to do so was in itself a great tribute to the financial affluence to which he had brought the Crown. But the prospect of a continuation of the campaign, and the probability of being obliged to

try and chastise Louis XI for his virtual repudiation of the
Treaty of Picquigny, induced the summons of a parliament
in January 1483. Money was granted, and the duke of
Gloucester, the earl of Northumberland, and Thomas,
Lord Stanley, received cordial commendations for their
services against the Scots. Gloucester indeed was given
exceptional grants with large powers south and north of
the Border. A new star, even though a northern one, had
risen high in the Yorkist firmament.

But on 9 April, Edward IV, after a short illness, died, not
yet forty-one years of age. For him, perhaps, it was a
crowning mercy, for most likely he had reached if not
passed his zenith as king. But for his family his premature
death spelt calamity.

Edward IV's achievements as man and king were not
small. In no sense born to the kingship, he was eighteen
years of age before his father even got to the point of
claiming the Crown. When his father and next eldest
brother died at Wakefield, Edward undertook no light
task in pressing home the cause that had fallen into his
hands. Press it home, however, he did, with resolution and
courage, and although he probably never would have
achieved his objective without the aid of the Nevilles,
certainly he was at no time a mere pawn in their hands. It
is clear enough now that however warily he may have had
to walk for years after his accession, his aim was untrammelled power for himself as king. In spite of all his difficulties, the vicissitudes he underwent, the reversals of
fortunes that were his lot, and of the very narrow margin
by which he escaped complete ruin in 1470, he did in fact
obtain his goal.

It was important for English history that he did do so.
The steady decline in the prestige and resources of the
monarchy since the end of the fourteenth century had
brought disaster and decadence in government, and had

made the civil wars not only possible but inevitable. The extreme weakness of the office of king under Henry VI had gravely jeopardized law and justice, administration, and economic development, and had reduced to a low ebb the position of England on the Continent. It was very necessary, if the government of England was to continue along its historic path, that the monarchy should be restored, re-invigorated, and set along lines which would ensure a far more efficient and vigorous government than Lancaster had ever been able to provide. For there was no alternative, either then or for long thereafter, to strong personal monarchy but some form or other of magnate conciliar government, with all its accompanying corruptions, dis-sensions, and administrative anarchy, such as had already been experienced in the time of Henry VI.

Edward IV supplied the remedy, and what he did went far to determine that the government of England would continue to be a monarchy in fact as well as in name, with-out involving the destruction of any of the established and by then traditional institutions. By the time Edward IV had finished his career, there was no over-mighty subject left in England. It was but the irony of history that others were to reap where he had sown. The foundations of what has commonly been called the 'New Monarchy' were laid not by Henry VII, but by Edward IV. For when, before very long, and against all probability, Henry Tudor came to acquire the Crown, he could not for many years do much more than follow the lines of goverment which had already been set by Edward IV. There was no alternative open to a landless and penniless refugee who had never before had any personal acquaintance with the practice of government or the arts of management. In spite of all, the work of the Yorkists was to receive its greatest justification from the success with which Henry VII followed their precedents.

IV

York Divided Against Itself

THE premature death of Edward IV, on 9 April, 1483, brought catastrophe to the House of York. It was easy enough to proclaim his eldest son King Edward V, to make preparations for his coronation, and to begin to think of his brother Richard, duke of York, as the heir-presumptive for many years to come. But both the boys, aged twelve and nine years respectively, were far too young and inexperienced to count for much themselves. Moreover, their father had been personally so overwhelmingly dominant for so many years that he inevitably left behind him a political power-vacuum. There was no one left at the centre, either eminent or powerful enough to ensure adequate stability or direction during what would necessarily be a long minority, or even perhaps two successive minorities should Edward V, reputedly not a robust boy, also die prematurely. The Nevilles had years ago finished their monarch-making careers; Clarence was dead; even Henry Bourchier, earl of Essex, had died five days before Edward IV. It was inevitable that the Queen Mother and her Woodville relatives would proceed to fill the vacuum, with or without the assistance of lesser figures, such as the dead king's Chamberlain and boon-companion, Lord Hastings; his Steward, Lord Stanley, and probably Bishop Morton of Ely, both of whom might well have other fish to fry as time went on. For Stanley had recently become the third husband[1] of no less equivocal a person than the Lady Margaret Beaufort, countess of Richmond,

[1] But see p. 113, n. 1 above.

whose only son, even if in exile, could scarcely have failed to rejoice at the turn of events; Bishop Morton, although he had served Edward IV, was originally Lancastrian in sympathy, and his experience in political intrigue and cunning in statecraft might not always be wholly devoted to the service of Edward V. Woodville ascendancy seemed inevitable in the circumstances but for the possible drastic intervention of the boy-king's surviving uncle, Richard, duke of Gloucester. Richard, now by far the most powerful magnate left in England, found himself suddenly in a position of disconcerting and indeed dangerous isolation. There was not any male member of the royal family left upon whom he could rely, and none at all older than himself (except Archbishop Bourchier). He had hitherto taken little part in government at the centre, but at all times from a very early age he had faithfully served his elder brother, had followed him in all his fortunes and fought by his side whenever occasion had required. He had risen steadily in his trust, and had been appointed to a series of posts of responsibility; his assistance had materially helped Edward through the crises of Warwick's and Clarence's defections. He had served the king loyally, but had committed no crime. He did not murder Prince Edward at Tewkesbury; he could have had no personal responsibility for the demise of Henry VI, who anyway had been sentenced to the penalties of attainder ten years before the sentence was carried out, if indeed it really was carried out; he had had nothing to do with the attainder of Clarence, of which he appears to have disapproved. Indeed, he had not been seen much at court since that event, and it may well be that the king's ruthless action on that occasion estranged Richard from him, whose loose morals and indulgent mode of life were certainly not to Richard's taste. A far more austere and disciplined character than his brother the king, Richard had lived quietly in the north, mostly at Middleham Castle, with his wife and their son Edward, for some ten years before Edward IV died, and had earned golden opinions as a wise and conscientious ruler of the north and the Marches, and recently as the chastiser of the Scots. When the news of the king's death reached him, Richard was in his thirty-first year, and was the ablest and most experienced soldier and administrator left in the realm.

But his personal isolation was extreme; he could not be sure that his just claim to the Protectorate during the minority would be recognized, nor how long he would last as Protector even if he ever took up such an office. On the other hand, he could expect the Woodvilles to do all they could to minimize his influence and power, and to prejudice the boy-king, who scarcely knew him at all, against him in all possible ways. Whatever else Richard would have to do, he would have to exert himself vigorously and at once. It seemed to him, therefore, that the first step he must take, in his own interests, in those of the boy-king himself, and of all the realm, was to remove his nephew from the custody of his Woodville relatives, and bring him under his own protection. There can be no doubt that he was, in all the circumstances, absolutely right to do so, and indeed received aid and advice in the matter from Lord Hastings in London, who had no desire to see the son and heir of York left wholly to the care of his maternal relatives.

As a precautionary move, it was only elementary prudence for Richard to take possession of the person of Edward V at Stoney Stratford on 30 April, whither he had been escorted from Ludlow en route for London by his senior maternal uncle and tutor, Anthony Woodville, Earl Rivers, by his half-brother Sir Richard Grey, and the treasurer of his Household as prince of Wales, Sir Thomas Vaughan. But in the meantime circumstances had changed materially. For the only other male descendant from Edward III of rank and importance left (apart from the Archbishop) had come forward and offered his support to

*The autographs of Edward V, Richard,
duke of Gloucester, and Henry Stafford,
duke of Buckingham (1483), together
with the mottoes of the two dukes
('Leyoulte me lie' and 'Souvente me souvene')*

(B.M. Vespasian MS. F XIII, fo. 123)

Richard in what might ensue. Henry Stafford, second
duke of Buckingham, had communicated with him and
had joined forces with him at Northampton on 29 April.
The intervention at Stoney Stratford on the next day,
therefore, did not come from Richard alone, but from the
two dukes jointly.

Buckingham, a man a year or two younger than Richard,
of royal lineage and proud of it, had not taken much part
in national affairs. He had no particular reason to love the
Yorkist branch of the royal family; the Staffords had been
pro-Lancastrian, and both his grandfather and father had
fallen in that cause. He loved the Woodvilles even less, for
when very young he had been obliged to accept in marriage

K

one of Queen Elizabeth's sisters and to make her his duchess, a *mésalliance* (in his eyes) which he had deeply resented. One would like to know what thoughts had raced through his mind when five years earlier he had been made High Steward for the express purpose of pronouncing sentence of death upon George, duke of Clarence. One Yorkist the less, and one so near to his detested sister-in-law's husband, could scarcely have been unwelcome to him.

There was therefore nothing particularly ominous about Richard's taking the boy-king into his possession, except perhaps for the Woodvilles. Earl Rivers, Sir Richard Grey, and also Sir Thomas Vaughan, it is true, were taken into custody and sent up for safe-keeping, out of harm's way, to one or another of Richard's northern castles. On hearing this news, Queen Elizabeth, with her other royal son, hastened into sanctuary at Westminster (as she had in 1470, but this time with elaborate preparations for a long stay); her eldest son by her first marriage and the most unpopular member of the family, now the marquis of Dorset, took to his heels, and his brother Edward Woodville conveniently sought without delay to implement the Council's decision to undertake naval operations in the Channel to deal with impending French attacks resulting from the break-down of amicable relations before Edward IV had died. Richard and Buckingham could escort the king up to London without further difficulty, and they entered the city, probably on 4 May. Richard was now speedily recognized as Protector and Defender of the realm, if indeed he had not already been, and he appointed a number of new ministers, and generally set the wheels of government moving. Preparations for the coronation of Edward V went ahead, and writs were issued on 13 May for a parliament to meet on 25 June, to which it was proposed to refer the question of the duration and powers of the Protectorate. The new Chancellor, the very reputable

John Russell, bishop of Lincoln, could put in hand a draft
for his opening speech for the parliament. But, as it turned
out, he was obliged to re-write it before very long, for no
parliament in the name of Edward V was to meet that
year or in any year, nor any parliament at all that year,
and the only coronation that year was not to be Edward
V's.

It is difficult indeed to say just at what stage in these
proceedings Richard finally made up his mind to oust his
nephews and obtain the Crown for himself. It is reasonably
certain that no such project could have entered his head
before the news of Edward IV's death reached him shortly
after 9 April; it is possible but far from certain that some
such scheme was mooted at the conference he had privately
with Buckingham and their intimate advisers at Northampton on the night of 29 April — possible but very
unlikely that as yet he would confide to that extent in
Buckingham, even if the project had as yet been formed in
his own mind. The armed forces which the two dukes took
with them to London were not large, and undoubtedly,
whatever plan may have been in mind, they had to walk
very warily indeed for some time. The question of what
Lord Hastings and his friends, in association or not with
the Woodvilles (or such of them as were still at liberty)
would do, was all-important. True, by 10 June, Richard
was writing up to York for armed men to be sent down to
London to support him against contingencies, but in fact
all decisive steps had been taken before they actually
arrived. Many doubts and uncertainties had to be resolved
before Richard could have seen very far ahead, and the
first overt act by him which seems to reveal to us his
intention to usurp came on 13 June, when he procured the
arrest and death of William, Lord Hastings. Whether
Hastings was summarily beheaded on a barely credible
charge of treason, or was (as a contemporary chronicler
specifically states with much greater probability) in fact

killed whilst other councillors were being arrested, is immaterial. Doubtless Richard had secretly sounded Hastings as to his attitude towards a possible change in the succession, and finding his response uncongenial, had determined that he must at all costs and at once be removed from the arena. For Hastings was a dangerous man with whom to have to reckon. Able and experienced in war and government, and a close intimate of Edward IV, he was not only the late king's Chamberlain but also Captain of Calais, and still more disquieting from Richard's point of view, he had (as we now know), been for years building up a formidable body of indentured retainers, men of substance with hosts of followers behind them, who had contracted to serve him in peace and war, and who, once they could be mobilized, would have made the prospect for Richard highly dubious. Of course, Hastings was in no way unique in having such retainers — it was the common practice of the period — but for Richard the hazards in the circumstances were too great to be risked. Hastings had to be eliminated without delay if the way for usurpation were to be kept open. Actually such men as Hastings had with him in London promptly accepted service at once with another 'good lord' — a very good lord as it seemed to them at the moment — none other than Henry, duke of Buckingham.

It is quite possible, even probable, that Richard could not have seen his way ahead at all, until such time as he saw a plausible excuse for setting aside his nephews. We do not know when he first knew of the story of Edward IV's alleged pre-contract of marriage; it may well be that he first heard of it from Bishop Stillington[1] after Edward IV

---

[1] Robert Stillington had been keeper of the Privy Seal 1460–67, and Chancellor 1467–1470 and in 1471. But at about the time Clarence met his end, he was imprisoned in the Tower for a time by Edward IV. The reasons for this disgrace are not known; all we know is that in his subsequent pardon he was said to have spoken words 'prejudicial to the king and his state'. He was not restored to favour by Edward IV, received no appreciable reward from Richard III, and was to be imprisoned again by Henry VII.

was dead, and if this was so he is not likely to have been told it before his arrival in London about 4 May. According to this allegation, Edward IV had entered into a pre-contract of marriage (with strictly dishonourable intentions) with the late Lady Eleanor Butler, a lady of repute who fortunately had been dead some fifteen years, and who had been the daughter of the famous John Talbot, earl of Shrewsbury, and the widow of Sir Thomas Butler. Edward therefore had not been canonically free to marry Elizabeth Woodville (Eleanor having been alive at that time); his marriage had been invalid and all his children were bastards. If this were so, and since Clarence was dead and attainted, the pure word of Yorkist legitimism could leave no doubt but that the inheritance of the Crown must lawfully reside in the person of Richard himself. Nothing then remained to do but to adapt to the prevailing circumstances the procedure which the earl of March had followed in 1461.

The story was plausible on the face of it; Edward IV's amorous propensities had been notorious enough to make it credible; all the parties concerned were dead; it could neither be proved nor disproved. Richard himself is unlikely to have invented it, and he may even have believed it (though whether the Church would have officially pronounced the children bastards had it been asked to adjudicate legally upon the point is another matter). The story may have been true, for what it was worth, or perhaps Stillington invented it and expected to thrive greatly should Richard act thereupon.

At any rate here to hand for Richard to use if he wanted was the one and only theory which could effect an immediate change in the succession, whilst upholding those principles of legitimism upon which York had come to the throne twenty-two years earlier. It would have been hard indeed for Richard to have attained the Crown without the aid of some such story; if it were not true, then it had to be invented, for without legitimism York was lost. Even so, it would be a mistake to think of Richard as a mere opportunist. The great prize which his eldest brother had won in 1461, and had fought against such odds to retain, was not lightly to be entrusted to the hazards of a long minority. The risk that advantage might be taken of the situation in other quarters was very great. All that York had achieved might be cast away if its maintenance depended upon an unknown and totally inexperienced boy-king and his grasping maternal relatives, by now intermingled among a dozen or more noble houses. Besides, Richard must needs think of his own future. 'For well he saw he could not live, unless he were king; that there was no safety but in sovereignty.'[1]

Once resolved on his objective, Richard's moves were as masterly as they were rapid, and he achieved his purpose without overt opposition. By 13 June, Hastings was no more; on 16 June Edward V's brother, Richard, duke of York, was extracted from his mother's care in Westminster Abbey by no less reputable a person than his great-uncle the venerable Thomas Bourchier, cardinal archbishop of Canterbury, and sent to join his brother in the Tower. There was nothing sinister about such a move. The Tower was still a royal residence, and it was customary for the kings to lodge there, pending their coronation procession thence to the Abbey. It was therefore only fitting that the two brothers should be together in preparation for such an event.

But by 22 June the story of their bastardy was being put about; on 23 and 24 June Buckingham justified his reputation for eloquence by his harangues to assembled lords and citizens of London. By 26 June Richard, duke of Gloucester, was being presented with a petition to assume the Crown as the rightful heir by 'election of us the three estates of this land'. Before that day was over, he had

[1] Sir William Cornwallis, *The Enconium of Richard III*, (c. 1603).

accepted this invitation, been acclaimed King Richard III, and taken his seat on the marble chair in Westminster Hall towards which his father Richard, duke of York, had stretched out his hand in vain in 1460.

On 5 July there was indeed a procession from the Tower to the Abbey, but it was not one suitable for Edward IV's 'bastards' to take part in. For the coronation next day was that of their uncle Richard III, in the presence of almost all the lords temporal and their ladies and of the lords spiritual, celebrated with the utmost magnificence and dignity and performed by the proper archiepiscopal hands.[1] Everybody who was anybody was there; the Lady Margaret Beaufort, Baroness Stanley and countess of Richmond was there, duly attendant upon the new Queen Ann — a Neville had come to the throne after all. But Elizabeth Woodville and her daughters stayed in the sanctuary part of the building. Her eldest brother Anthony and her son Sir Richard Grey were not there either; for they, along with Sir Thomas Vaughan, were no longer in a position to leave Pontefract Castle for any purpose; Yorkist 'reason of state' had caught up with them. The two princes stayed in the Tower of London — permanently.

We can be sure of that, but what actually happened to them, no one has ever been able to ascertain. No evidence has survived to prove how or when they died; but the probability is that they did not die a natural death and that they were dead before March, 1484. It is probable that they were progressively withdrawn from public view, and certain that they eventually disappeared altogether. The possibility of a natural death (which Richard III never dared reveal) cannot be entirely excluded, but their

---

[1] It is not surprising that Thomas Bourchier, now of advanced years and who had crowned Edward IV and also Elizabeth Woodville, and was destined to crown Henry VII and to marry him to Elizabeth's daughter, is reported to have showed some reluctance to crown Richard III and Ann Neville, but to do so was an official duty which he could scarcely avoid unless he were to resign the archbishopric or flee abroad.

Queen Ann Neville and Richard III
(*The Rous Roll, loc. cit.*, pls. 58 and 59)

death by assassination is far more likely. More than one person then or later had a motive for removing them, but the person who had the most immediate motive and every opportunity was unquestionably Richard III himself. Bastardization was all very well for the moment, but once again 'stone dead hath no fellow'. Certainly Henry Tudor would have had little or no chance of the throne if either of them had been alive in 1485, and could have been relied upon to remedy Richard III's oversight if need had arisen, but it is altogether improbable that in fact either of them was still alive then. Indeed, it seems most unlikely that Henry VII himself was ever able to discover what actually had happened to them; at any rate, he made no attempt to publish any explanation of the mystery until circumstances years later forced him to try to convince the public that the princes really had been murdered in the time of Richard III. The best he could do then was to promulgate an alleged but quite unconvincing 'confession' by a man (Sir James Tyrell) who was about to lose (or had already lost) his head, not for murder but for treason to Henry VII himself.

But nothing was seen of the princes after the spring of 1484 at latest; true there were rumours that they had been put to death as early as the autumn of 1483, and these rumours played an important part in the course of events at that time. Moreover, there is some reason to believe not only that they were dead, but that their mother knew they were dead, before 1 March, 1484.[1] As for the manner of their death, nothing is known with any certainty. The discovery of bones 'under the stairs' at the Tower in 1674, commonly supposed to lend colour to Sir James Tyrell's story of their suffocation and burial by dead of night, etc. as reported by Sir Thomas More in 1513, does not help us very much. For it cannot be proved when those bones were buried, or by whom, or even whether they are bones of boys at all, nor with any precision what the ages were of the persons whose bones they are. Many rumours circulated contemporaneously, or nearly so, as to the manner of their death. The bones which had been discovered some thirty years earlier than those 'under the stairs' immured in a room near the apartments which the princes occupied, may equally well be theirs, and indeed even more probably, for one contemporary chronicler, a Burgundian, specifically included in his catalogue of rumours the allegation that the princes had been walled up in a room and left to starve.[2] The utter silence that fell upon them would

---

[1] Polydore Vergil, writing years later, dropped the remark that the envoys sent by Richard III to persuade Elizabeth Woodville to come to terms at first prejudiced their mission by alluding to the death of her sons. Whilst such a remark cannot be deemed conclusive evidence, its inclusion in the context seems pointless unless there were some substance in it.

[2] J. Molinet, *Chroniques des ducs de Bourgogne*, ed. J. A. Buchon, Paris, 1827 II, 402.

certainly be more comprehensible if this was what really happened, for in such circumstances extremely few people need ever have known the truth. Probably in any event no one who had known the facts survived the battle of Bosworth. No one need ever have known exactly what happened, except the person responsible; and if, as is most probable, the boys were not alive at the time of that battle, it is very unlikely that any one would have taken responsibility for their death except Richard III himself. But the fact is that unless some much more conclusive evidence comes to light, we shall never know with any certainty what the fate of the princes in the Tower really was. The weight of suspicion against Richard III must remain extremely heavy, but of proof there is none at present.

It is possible that Richard could have afforded to let his nephews subsist indefinitely; officially they were now bastards, out of the succession, and too powerless themselves to give any trouble. But early and serious threats to his security would inevitably have turned his thoughts in a direction which he perhaps had not contemplated at first. He was not by nature of a murderous disposition, but just as another usurper, Henry IV, had by 1400 found his hand forced by the inexorable pressure of circumstances to eliminate his cousin Richard II, so, most likely, Richard III discovered in 1483–4 that harsh facts were not to be evaded by mere theories. They had to be met with equally harsh deeds.

The problem of how to retain the Crown he had won so easily, by such masterly timing and subtle moves, beset Richard III from the start of his reign. He had secured acquiescence and even public support for his accession from the great majority of the peerage, but to build up a personnel upon whom he could rely for loyal service and the manifold tasks of government was less easy. He needs must reward Buckingham at once for services rendered and to be rendered (as he thought) with honorific posts and grants with large powers and profits, especially in those Welsh regions in which Buckingham already possessed extensive interests, but he can scarcely have wished to encourage the idea that there was another king-maker come to power. He lost no time in providing Buckingham (and for that matter his own brother-in-law John de la Pole, duke of Suffolk) with a rival duke in the person of John Howard, now created duke of Norfolk,[1] and made him Admiral of England. But he could not find many great names with which to fill the chief offices in his government. Henry Percy, earl of Northumberland, could be mollified to some extent by being allowed to succeed to much of Richard's own position in the north; he could retain Bishop Russell as Chancellor; he could replace Hastings as Chamberlain by a faithful adherent — Francis, Viscount Lovell, and retain Lord Stanley close to his own eye as Steward, but otherwise he was obliged to use for the most part commoners and lesser men, many of whom had served him as duke of Gloucester, who were reliable because they depended entirely upon him for advancement. The Tyrells, Catesbys, and Ratcliffes who figured prominently in the régime, even if they did not exactly rule all England under him, at least did much to keep the wheels of government moving.

Having established an administration, written to most of the rulers of Europe to inform them of the fact of his accession, apprised the garrison of Calais that they had acted too precipitately in taking an oath of allegiance to Edward V, and having sent an envoy to the duke of Brittany to try and persuade him to hand over Henry of Richmond to him for 'safer custody', Richard felt able to

---

[1] The fact that John Howard was created duke of Norfolk on 28 June, 1483 does not necessarily imply that Richard, duke of York, who had been made duke of Norfolk in 1477, after he had been married to Ann Mowbray, heiress of the Mowbray dukes of Norfolk, was already dead by that date, or that Howard had anything to do with the death of either of the princes.

set out on an elaborate progress through the central counties. In August, he could create his son and heir prince of Wales, and soon after invest him as such in York Minster. He could learn with complacency of the death of Louis XI of France on 30 August. But by 11 October, when he was at Lincoln, he received the much more disagreeable and indeed staggering news that the duke of Buckingham was up in open rebellion against him, and that several uprisings had already occurred in some southern and south-western shires in favour of Edward V.

It is difficult to perceive the motives of Buckingham in making so rapid a defection from Richard. Such a *volte-face* was of course well within the king-making and un-making tradition, but in order to have staged a rebellion by early October, he must surely have decided upon his course many weeks earlier, so that Richard could scarcely have been crowned king before Buckingham's thoughts must have turned in a double-crossing direction. So extremely rapid a change of front suggests, indeed, that possibly he had intended to set up Richard only in order to knock him over later as soon as possible. His own offer of aid to Richard back in April becomes highly suspect in the light of these events. It is possible that Buckingham in fact had remained Lancastrian in sentiment all along, in the tradition of his own family, and that his fundamental purpose had been to procure the destruction of the House of York. He can hardly have thought to restore Edward V, for he announced him dead before the rebellion broke (come to that, he himself had had at least an opportunity for making sure of the boys' demise after Richard had left London and before he himself had set out for Brecon). For a brief period he may have seriously thought of himself as a suitable supplanter, but at some stage he clearly plumped for Henry of Richmond, had entered into an agreement with him, and his rebellion was intended to be in co-operation with him.[1] Very likely the wily Bishop Morton, who had been arrested by Richard at the same time as Hastings and committed to Buckingham's custody at the latter's request, had a good deal to do with shaping the duke's plans. At Brecon Castle, Morton had ample opportunity for focusing the duke's mind upon the Lancastrian interest as represented by Henry.

But the rebellion was a fiasco. Few of Buckingham's Welsh tenants (among whom he was far from popular) would move; some of his neighbours prejudiced his chances; local floods impeded progress. Richard's countermoves were prompt and energetic; practically no fighting was involved at all, and All Souls' Day (2 November) saw the execution of Buckingham in the market place of Salisbury. Henry of Richmond emerged from Brittany only to return in haste as soon as the news broke.

The first attempt to unseat Richard III failed utterly. He could soon apply himself to the work of government, and seek to continue to provide what York was expected to provide — 'politique reule and governance'. By 23 January, 1484, he could at last meet his first (and as it turned out his only) parliament, which had been postponed because of the rebellions. It sat for only a month, and its principal business was to ratify the *fait accompli* of the accession, with suitable and impressive formulae, to attaint Buckingham and some ninety participants in the recent risings, including Henry Tudor, Jasper Tudor, Margaret Beaufort, and the marquess of Dorset, and Bishop Morton (who had fled to the Continent) for good measure. But he would not proceed to extremes against the Lady Margaret Beaufort, whose implication in the recent plots was undoubted; he deprived her of her lands, only to give them into the custody of her husband

[1] It should be remembered that Henry of Richmond's mother Margaret Beaufort was at one time married to Buckingham's uncle Henry Stafford (see p. 113 above).

Lord Stanley for life, with reversion to himself and his heirs.

Some useful but not remarkable statutes were passed, mostly on the initiative of the government — which was to be the predominant source of legislation henceforward for a very long time. The statutes were of somewhat minor importance, except for a prohibition upon the exaction of those benevolences which had been such an unpopular feature of Edward IV's later years.

But, by and large, Richard III continued the administrative work of Edward IV, especially in the sphere of finance. He had similar councillors, and made extensive use of his secretary armed with the signet seal as the immediate instrument of his decisions. In his ducal days he had employed useful administrators, some of whom had at one time also had experience in Edward IV's service, and who now once again came into royal administration, and he himself had had many years' experience in government, administration, and estate management. He brought the profits of his own duchy of Gloucester to swell the royal revenues, and soon had a fine crop of forfeitures to add. He maintained Edward IV's use of the Chamber of the Household as a finance office of major importance, and applied the same methods of estate management as Edward IV had adopted. He could have a survey made of the organization of the royal revenues and contemplate an overhaul of the whole system in the interests of efficiency and greater net profit. He had views on the organization of a Council for the Northern parts towards Scotland (a matter in which he was highly expert), on the judicial work of the Council, on the organization of the Admiralty, and on other matters, which were to be substantially followed by his successor.

There is no doubt that Richard III was fully competent to follow and maintain the Yorkist tradition of improved government, and in the long run his usurpation might have justified itself on that ground, and the new monarchy

might have remained purely Yorkist in name and character as well as in origins.

By March 1484, the general auspices seemed favourable
to Richard, and the likelihood that he might be upset by
some rival had receded. By 1 March he had even succeeded
in coming to terms with Elizabeth Woodville, who, notwithstanding all that she must have known or guessed by
then, not only agreed to come out of sanctuary with her
daughters, but also promised to persuade her (presumably)
only surviving son, the marquess of Dorset, to abandon
Henry of Richmond and come home into Richard's good
lordship. It was a notable triumph for Richard, but of
course there was no visible future for Elizabeth or her
daughters unless they accepted Richard's overtures.

But thereafter his fortunes declined. A shattering blow
to his hopes was delivered by the sudden death in mid-
April of his heir-apparent and only legitimate child. It is
probable that this unexpected catastrophe unnerved him,
and impaired both his judgment and his resolution. When
within a year his queen, Ann, also died, his prospect of
being able to maintain the Yorkist dynasty became
exceedingly doubtful. He lacked henceforth the dynast's
incentive for the ruthlessness which might have saved the
situation which was soon to arise. In the circumstances he
may have under-estimated the threat which Henry of
Richmond now represented in much higher degree than
before. He could scarcely develop any great enthusiasm
for his only two possible male heirs-presumptive.[1] He
could marry again no doubt (if only he could find a suitable
wife — his bastardized niece could hardly come into that
category), but years must necessarily elapse before much
safety in an heir-apparent could possibly be found. He

---

[1] These were Edward, earl of Warwick, born 1475, the son of his late
brother George, duke of Clarence and Isabel Neville, who was to be
beheaded by Henry VII in 1499, and John, earl of Lincoln, born 1464, the
son of his sister Elizabeth and John de la Pole, duke of Suffolk, who was
killed at the battle of Stoke in 1487 (see p. 159 below).

Richard III
Painting at Windsor Castle. Artist unknown.

might have reduced some of Henry of Richmond's chances by marrying off all of his nieces (bastards or not) to other men, but he failed to do so. His actions against Margaret Beaufort might have been far more drastic than they were, and he might have put the whole Stanley family into more constraint than he did. He could fulminate against Henry, could almost but not quite succeed in extracting him from

Edward, prince of Wales, son of Richard III and Queen Ann

(*The Rous Roll, loc. cit.*, pl. 64)

the boundaries of Brittany; but he could not prevent his escape to the safer refuge of France, and apparently did not even attempt to procure his assassination. He could exact heavy security for good behaviour from a number of his subjects of uncertain fidelity, but parchment bonds proved no substitute for loyalty.

Even so, when at length the issue came to be brought to trial by battle at Bosworth field on 22 August, 1485, Richard III, according to the odds, should have won through. There was no soldier of his ability and experience

L

in the opposite camp; Henry himself had never fought a battle, and had to rely on the veteran Lancastrian earl of Oxford as his Captain-General to give a lead to his unpredictable troops. Richard was well-supported by captains and men superior in numbers, few of whom could afford to lose the battle if they could help it. It is a tolerable certainty that he would in fact have won, and actually was within a hair's breadth of doing so, but for the decisive treachery of the Stanleys and their men, and for the indecisive inaction of his old rival Henry Percy, earl of Northumberland.

Richard III was at Nottingham when news reached him on 11 August that Henry, with a small French supporting force, had arrived in Milford Haven[1] on 7 August. Richard had good grounds for expecting that Henry would not succeed in getting through Wales into the heart of England, but these expectations were not fulfilled. Although some threats to his progress existed, in fact Henry was able to land just before sunset to occupy Dale, to proceed at break of day to Haverfordwest and then to march unmolested through Carmarthenshire and Cardiganshire to Aberystwyth, Machynlleth, and Newtown, and so to Shrewsbury by about 15 August. Continuation of this advance towards Lichfield brought Richard out of Nottingham, probably on 19 August, and down to Leicester. On Sunday, 21 August, he moved up with substantial forces to within striking distance of his enemies, and camped for the night, probably at

[1] Most modern identifications of the landing place are inaccurate. The landing was made *in* Milford Haven, but not at (the modern town of) Milford Haven, which did not then exist. Polydore Vergil stated explicitly that Henry entered Milford Haven, forthwith landed, and took first a place called Dale, where, he had heard, forces had been stationed during the previous winter to oppose his landing. The first cove in the Haven on the northern side is in fact Mill Bay, on the eastern side of St. Ann's Head, 2 miles south of Dale. Common sense and local tradition support the belief that this was the actual landing-place. Richard III's information, disclosed in a letter of his dated 11 August, that the landing had been made at Angle on the southern side of the Haven, may be explained by the probability that a detachment landed there to advance on Pembroke and Tenby castles. Cf. J. F. Rees, *Milford Haven* (1954) and H. T. Evans, *Wales and the Wars of the Roses* (1915).

Sutton Cheney, about two miles south of Market Bosworth.

By the pure military chances, Richard III should have won the battle next morning without much difficulty. He himself was an experienced and capable general; he commanded, or seemed to command, superior forces; he occupied a hill-site overlooking his adversaries, who perforce had to fight up-hill to reach his ranks; he was the king in possession. The efforts of John de Vere, earl of Oxford, on Henry's right, to attack and entice downhill John Howard, duke of Norfolk's force on Richard's left, were unsuccessful, although Howard himself lost his life at an early stage. It was Richard's own impatience to end the struggle by personal combat with Henry that brought the decisive climax; his impatience was indeed well-grounded, for he had every reason to distrust the equivocal hoverings of Sir William Stanley and Thomas, Lord Stanley on the flanks of the two main armies, and he could not but notice that Henry Percy, earl of Northumberland, in a commanding position on his own right flank, had made no overt move against the Stanleys' menacing forces. A quick thrust at Henry of Richmond himself would still, if successful, have saved the day, as by then no other device could. He was not to know for certain, no matter what he suspected, that both the Stanleys had already secretly met and communed with Henry, and were merely waiting an opportunity to intervene on Henry's side, provided that they could be sure that would be the winning side. Richard's dash forward with a small force to engage Henry and his immediate guards was indeed very nearly successful and Henry was brought into great danger, but it gave the decisive opportunity to Sir William Stanley and his men, who raced across the field to the rescue, routed the attack, and killed Richard, who fought until he could no more.[1]

---

[1] No very satisfactory contemporary, and therefore no modern, account of the battle exists. The above is merely a summary of what appear to have been the crucial facts.

So it was that the paper crown which had mocked the trunkless head of Edward III's great-grandson Richard of York turned, after twenty-five years, into a golden one rolling among the bushes of Bosworth Field, and that the sword-gashed body of York's fourth and last son lay stretched naked and exposed across the back of a horse at the last.

The House of York divided against itself had not stood. Nonetheless, the blood of Mortimer, Neville, and Woodville, as well as that of Plantagenet and Valois, of Lancaster and Beaufort, would come to mingle in the veins of the third generation of Tudor since the days when a certain Welsh squire had lain his head in the lap of a lonesome Queen Dowager.

V

The Heir Assumptive

IT is salutary for historians who may be prone to assume the inevitability of the Tudor story, to remember how extremely improbable it was in reality that Henry Tudor, attainted earl of Richmond, would ever mount the throne of England, or marry Elizabeth, the eldest daughter of Edward IV and Elizabeth Woodville.

Henry had been born in Pembroke Castle on 28 January, 1457, the posthumous son of Edmund Tudor, (who had been created earl of Richmond in 1453 by his half-brother, Henry VI), and of Margaret Beaufort, great-grand-daughter of John of Gaunt and Katherine Swynford. His mother was not quite fourteen years of age when he was born, and his father died of natural causes in 1456. The prospects for Henry became very dubious as the fortunes of Lancaster declined, and indeed, soon came to turn on the extent to which he might come to be linked with the rise of the fortunes of the friends of York. For a few years he was brought up under the protection of his uncle Jasper, earl of Pembroke, at Pembroke Castle. But on 30 September, 1461, that castle fell to the Yorkists, and although Jasper got away, Henry did not, and on 12 February, 1462, the custody and future marriage of the boy was granted (in consideration for the sum of £1,000) to Sir William Herbert — Lord Herbert of Raglan as he had recently become — a man rising fast in the service and confidence of Edward IV. Henry was committed to the care of Herbert's wife, Ann Devereux, and his education proceeded under the aegis of the staunch Yorkist househo at Raglan and probably elsewhere, for nearly ten years. During these impressionable years, we may be sure, he imbibed sound Yorkist ideas, and most probably, but for the defection of Warwick and the re-adeption of Henry VI, he would have become his guardian's son-in-law, for it was the expressed intention of Lord Herbert (who became earl of Pembroke in 1468) to marry him to his own eldest daughter Maud. What would have happened to the history of England, of Tudor England and its historians, if Henry had settled down as a respectable Yorkist partisan, and perhaps trusted counsellor of Edward IV and maybe Richard III, tantalizes the imagination. However, the fates, by a prolonged series of unlikely turns and twists, determined otherwise. Warwick did defect from Edward IV, and procured the decapitation of his serious rival Lord Herbert after Edgecote in 1469; the restoration of Henry's half-uncle Henry VI in 1470 seemed for a short time to put an entirely different complexion upon Henry Tudor's prospects, which radically changed again and took on a more ominous hue as soon as Edward IV contrived to win his way back to the throne. For after Barnet and Tewkesbury, with Henry VI and his son Edward gone beyond recall, Henry Tudor, in 1471, suddenly became at the age of fourteen a vastly more important young man than he had ever yet been. As the male representative of the senior Beaufort line, he at once began to look very much like a possible heir of Lancaster. It is somewhat unlikely that in the changed circumstances, he would have continued for long to enjoy the freedom of the Welsh or any other countryside, if his uncle Jasper had not been able to pick him up in the course of his withdrawal through Wales after Tewkesbury, and to take him with him when he eventually sailed away from Tenby.

Even then uncle and nephew were forced by the weather to abandon their intention of seeking refuge with Louis XI of France, and instead were forced to find asylum with

Sir William Herbert, earl of Pembroke, and his wife Ann Devereux, kneel before Edward IV. Before 1462.

(John Lydgate, *Troy Book*, B.M. Royal MS. 18 D. II, fo. 6)

Francis II, duke of Brittany, who, eager as he was to secure such useful pawns, was far more exposed to diplomatic and other pressures from the Yorkists than the king of France.

It was remarkable that the continous pressure which Edward IV and Richard III brought to bear upon Brittany from that date onwards never quite succeeded in achieving the surrender of Henry. Very remarkable indeed, for twice he escaped Yorkist clutches by a hair's breadth. In June 1476, Duke Francis agreed to surrender the prize, and Henry was actually on his way to a Yorkist future, when at the last minute the surrender was countermanded. In June 1484, Richard III's blandishments of the Chancellor of Brittany, at a time when the duke himself was ill and incapacitated, were on the very point of success, and would have succeeded, if the ubiquitous Bishop Morton, then in refuge in Flanders, had not got wind of the plot and had not warned Henry in the nick of time to enable him to escape into France. By then Louis XI was dead, but the regency of Anne of Beaugency eagerly welcomed him and soon assisted him to weave the plot which ripened in August, 1485.

By then Henry had reached his twenty-seventh year, but had never fought or even seen a battle, and his chances of defeating so seasoned a warrior and campaigner as Richard III, would have been slight in the extreme, if Henry had not been in the fortunate position of being able to rely for military skill and experience upon two capable captains (upon whom indeed he was to rely for the rest of their lives) — his uncle Jasper, who had began his fighting at the first battle of St Albans thirty years earlier; and by a highly unlikely turn of events, John de Vere III, thirteenth earl of Oxford, whose grandfather had fought at Agincourt, whose father had been executed by Edward IV in 1462, and whose own adventures had been striking. De Vere had helped to restore Henry VI, had fought at Barnet and survived, had seized St Michael's Mount in 1473, been captured, confined in Hammes Castle for ten years, had not only escaped from there in 1484 to join Henry but had also brought over with him the governor of that fortress. Without the assistance of these two veterans, it is difficult to see how Henry could either have risked the invasion of 1485, or have survived thereafter. For even the treachery of the Stanleys and the neutrality of Henry Percy at Bosworth were based upon a close estimate of the military chances.

Even so, Henry's expedition of August 1485 was a desperate venture, and probably the truth of the matter was that he could not afford to wait any longer if the attempt were to be made at all. The abortive nature of the effort of October 1483, and the speedy execution of Buckingham, had exposed the cause to ridicule; if Richard III survived too long he might well become too firmly entrenched to be easily dislodged; by the summer of 1485 circumstances had brought a goodly band of exiles around him in France, who could scarcely have retained their enthusiasm and hopes indefinitely; the government of France might not always countenance the plot; Henry himself by then had been fourteen years away from Wales, and scarcely ever set foot in England at any time, or at best only for a very brief and long passed-period.[1] Even Welsh memories and English pedigrees grow thin in time if un-nourished by personal presences. Moreover, the longer the delay, the more doubtful it would become whether he would ever be able to fulfil his oath, taken publicly in 1483, to marry Elizabeth of York if he succeeded, and failure to have been able to do that would have lost to him permanently much actual and prospective Yorkist sympathy. He himself in his younger days had narrowly escaped being married off to Maud Herbert; at

---

[1] He is known to have spent a short time in England during the restoration of Henry VI, to whom he may have been presented.

another time to a daughter of Warwick. Elizabeth of York, for her part, might not have remained available by 1485. Her father had intended that she should cement the French treaty by marrying the Dauphin; by 1485, with Richard III's queen and son dead, and Elizabeth Woodville come to terms with him, there was no knowing how long she would remain *femme sole*. Richard III might not have been able to marry her himself, but could certainly have married her off to someone else at any time if he had exerted himself (just as Henry himself later on was to arrange matters to his satisfaction in respect of the young ladies who were by then his wife's sisters). So doubtful became the matrimonial prospects, that Henry turned his thoughts at one time back in the direction of one of his former guardian's daughters. But in spite of all, Henry did in fact contrive to win the battle of Bosworth, the Crown, and in due course, the hand of Elizabeth of York.

Whatever Yorkist principles Henry may have learnt in the Herbert household at Raglan or Pembroke, legitimism was hardly one of them; or at any rate, this was not the principle on which he persuaded himself and others that he was king of England the day before Bosworth. There was no clear rule of inheritance upon which Henry Tudor could claim the Crown in 1485. If the Yorkist principle of legitimism as assumed in 1460–1 were valid, then even if all Edward IV's daughters were bastards, there were still several male Yorkists available whose legitimacy was not in doubt. The attainder of George, duke of Clarence, may have invalidated the claim of his son Edward, earl of Warwick, as Richard III had probably concluded after a very brief recognition of him as his heir presumptive after his own son's death. He could scarcely have avoided such a conclusion, otherwise it would have become difficult indeed to explain why he and not his own heir presumptive was king already. But that was not the end of the compli-

Queen Elizabeth, wife of Henry VII

Tomb-effigy in Westminster Abbey

cations. There were still the several sons of his sister
Elizabeth, duchess of Suffolk, headed by the eldest of
them, John, earl of Lincoln, to be reckoned with. But
Henry had not come to put a de la Pole on the throne. If

the Yorkist claim, whether in the male line by reason of attainder (although Henry himself was under attainder in 1485), or whether in the female line by reason of feminity, was to be set aside, and the Lancastrian line *had* been improperly displaced in 1460, who then was to be deemed the rightful heir of Lancaster in 1485? Certainly not Henry Tudor. The male line of Lancaster had come to an end at Tewkesbury, and if recourse were to be had to the Beaufort line, notwithstanding the circumstances of their legitimation and Henry IV's attempt at excluding them from the royal succession, it could only be in favour of a female, namely Lady Margaret Beaufort, Henry's own mother. But no one seriously thought of recognizing her as queen regnant. It was not for that purpose either that Henry had come.

In all these circumstances, Henry's own allusions to his rights by inheritance were inevitably kept extremely vague; and the less he said about the right of conquest the better, for he might be conquered himself for all he knew. Hence it was that his first parliament, when it came to the point, evaded all questions of legitimism and descent, all rights and wrongs, and with masterly simplicity, recognized the *fait accompli*, no more, no less. It was simply enacted, with the authority of parliament, that the inheritance of the Crown, with all the pre-eminence and dignity royal was, rested, and remained in the person of Henry (our now sovereign lord king), and in the heirs of his body, perpetually with the grace of God so to endure, and in none other.

As it turned out, this enactment of the king in the parliament of 1485–6, was to be no more than a statement of fact. The Crown *has* remained to the heirs of Henry's body ever since, though not in his heirs male only. Descent by heirs male alone would have brought the dynasty to an end in 1553. Henry VII's grand-daughters Mary and Elizabeth were to be recognized as queens regnant, and in

Lady Margaret Beaufort,
countess of Richmond and Derby

Tomb-effigy in Westminster Abbey

1603 the descendants of his daughter Margaret were to be
brought in from Scotland; some slight departures from the
strict line of descent were to be made in 1689, 1714, and
1936, but otherwise statute 1 Henry VII, c.1 has proved to
be a masterpiece of enunciation and prophecy.

But it was easier then to make prophetic enunciations
than to ensure the future. The ghosts of York could not be
laid by Act of Parliament, nor the offshoots of Plantagenet
be plucked out. The spectre of possible rivals, true or false
ones, haunted Henry VII all the days, and maybe the
nights, of his life, and inflamed the heated imagination of
his son after him; many guilty and innocent heads were to
roll so that the Tudors might sleep more easily in their
beds. Throughout the history of that dynasty, indeed, the
problem of the succession was never to be very far from the
thoughts of any member of it.

For Henry VII the problem remained acute for many
years, but his unceasing alertness and unflagging energy,
his mingled moderation and severity, his caution and
cunning, went far to solve the problem for his generation,
however fantastic the forms assumed by the spectre in his
life-time. He owed his success and ultimate triumph,
essentially perhaps, to the fact that there was no one left in
England prepared to support his rivals, who was powerful
enough to be able to evoke a repetition of the civil wars. He
owed it also to the fact that among the numerous foreign
potentates who at one time or another were glad to embarrass him by giving countenance to his possible rivals —
who could scarcely have survived for so long as they did
without such aid — the most inveterate and implacable
was a woman, avid of schemes but devoid of power or
much influence — Edward IV's sister, Margaret, mere
dowager duchess of Burgundy. Even she, when all her
schemes and patronage of impostors had come to naught,
felt it best to acquiesce in the *faits accomplis.* Henry's other
most persistent enemy, Margaret's step-daughter's hus-

band, Maximilian of Austria, proved to be too unstable
and too weak in resources to be able to do much practical
harm.

It was an odd, but not an inexplicable thing, that it was
not so much the genuine scions of York, as the impostors,
that gave Henry the most trouble, and that it was the very
impostors themselves who gave him the pretext and opportunity to dispose of the two potentially most dangerous of
those scions. The recognition in certain quarters, Irish in
the first instance in both cases, and spasmodically otherwise
foreign, of Lambert Simnel, initially as the earl of Warwick
and then as Edward VI; and of Perkin Warbeck, initially
as the earl of Warwick, then as Richard, duke of York, and
finally as Richard IV, retained an air of semi-comedy
throughout. The two lads themselves were of no personal
importance except as excellent actors who strutted and
ranted until at length the executioner's axe turned their
comic roles into tragedy. The pretensions of the one could
be ridiculed easily enough, for the earl of Warwick was
still alive and could be readily brought out of the Tower
and given an airing for the occasion. But it was not so easy
to refute the pretension of the other, for no one could show
proof that the younger Prince in the Tower was dead.
Nonetheless, Henry VII knew very well how to turn all
things to his profit, and the ultimate profit to him from
these remarkable impostures was that it gave him the lives
of both the principal nephews of Edward IV and Richard
III. The battle of Stoke, 16 June, 1487, which terminated
the Lambert Simnel *affaire*, saw the end of John de la Pole,
earl of Lincoln, the eldest son of Edward IV's sister
Elizabeth. He, although he had been received into good
grace by Henry VII (for the time being at any rate), had
foolishly and recklessly thrown in his lot with the rebels.
The long-drawn-out struttings of Perkin Warbeck, lasting
from 1491 to 1499, in Ireland, France, the Netherlands,
Scotland, and elsewhere, in the end brought a pretext for

the execution of George of Clarence's hapless son, Edward, earl of Warwick, who, having been an inmate of the Tower continuously (except for one day in 1487) since 1485, was scarcely in a position, mental or physical, to be a serious rival to anyone. But Tudor reason of state, like the Yorkist before it, had to have its victims.

The Warbeck episode brought down also no less a person than Sir William Stanley, Henry's rescuer and crown-bestower at Bosworth, and his mother's brother-in-law. How far Stanley had really capped his treachery to Richard III with treason to Henry VII remains problematical, but at least the decapitation of his own Chamberlain of the Household demonstrated unequivocally that Henry had no intention of shutting his eyes at hankerings after the White Rose among his own circle, even if in this instance he could only make an example at the cost of rejoicing the shade of Richard III himself.

The execution of Warwick in 1499 meant that the White Rose passed to the deceased John de la Pole's eldest brother, Edmund, earl of Suffolk, who could then claim to be the true heir of York, and if (as proved to be the case) he was to have no heirs of his own, his claim would after his death pass to his brothers and their heirs in succession. But some of these gentlemen were to prove from Henry's point of view, elusive. Suffolk, although promptly pardoned by Henry for a simple private murder which he had committed, took offence at the procedure adopted, and in the summer of 1499 fled from England to Flanders, not a little intoxicated by the heady scent of the highly dangerous White Rose. He spent some time with a certain Sir James Tyrell, then the governor of Guisnes, near Calais. He was, however, persuaded in due course to return amicably, and along with his brothers remained in Henry's good grace, only to flee again with his younger brother Richard, in the summer of 1501. His efforts at obtaining help from Maximilian, then king of the Romans and heir to the

Empire, and other possible supporters, went unrewarded, but the ominous potentiality of this conspiracy seriously perturbed Henry, as well it might, for now it was not a matter of having to deal with an imposter, but with the legitimate heir of the Yorkists. His espionage service soon brought him disquieting intelligence of the plot's ramifications at home. Suffolk's next eldest brother,[1] William de la Pole, his cousin by marriage Lord William Courteney, son of the earl of Devon, and other gentlemen alleged to be implicated, found themselves imprisoned, and a number of others were executed. Among them was Sir James Tyrell, who had been a faithful follower of Edward IV and of Richard III before being taken into favour by Henry VII. Tyrell, before his head fell on 6 May, 1502, was alleged by Henry to have confessed to the murder of the Princes in the Tower some eighteen years earlier. It is not clear why Tyrell should have immortalized his fame or infamy in this way, but then he could not have foreseen the future embalming power of Thomas More and William Shakespeare. The fact was that Henry VII had reached a point in his fortunes at which the laying of as many Yorkist ghosts as possible had become a matter of urgency. For by that date the succession in the male line to himself had come to depend upon the life of one boy not yet eleven years of age, and not a particularly robust boy at that. His eldest son Arthur had died on 2 April; his third son Edmund had died two years earlier; and now only his

---

[1] The publication of vol. XII, part 1, of *The Complete Peerage* (1953), Appendix I, has thrown fresh light on the sons of Elizabeth and John de la Pole, duke of Suffolk. It appears that there were seven of them altogether. The second son, Edward was dead before 1485, the third died young, the fourth, Humphrey, was a cleric and a country rector who died shortly before 1513; there was a sixth son Geoffrey, about whom little is known. But the interesting fact which emerges, and which is contrary to the commonly accepted view, is that William, not Richard, was the fifth son, and that Richard was the seventh and youngest son. The fact that William was the next heir after John helps to explain the fact (also contrary to received beliefs) that he never left the Tower for the rest of the many years of his life. See p. 162 below.

M

second son Henry, and two daughters, alone remained to uphold the dynasty. He could no longer afford to leave the mystery of the fate of the Princes without a plausible solution, and Tyrell's arrest for treason gave him almost his last opportunity for a 'confession', for Tyrell was one of the very few men, possibly by then the only one, who had been at all prominent in Richard III's entourage and still survived. It was a good story, too, and, with the aid of the then future dramatists and propagandists, survived the centuries, until modern historical criticism has exposed its essential incredibility.

Henry's diplomatic efforts at securing the person of Suffolk were unremitting for years, and involved the bringing of economic pressure to bear upon Philip, duke of Burgundy, in whose territories Suffolk had found refuge and some encouragement. His efforts were of no avail until chance in the form of an unlikely storm brought Philip and his wife Joanna involuntarily to the shores of England whilst they were voyaging to Castile, of which realm Joanna was the heiress. Henry's politeness and hospitality towards his unexpected guests were extreme and prolonged — prolonged until Philip at length agreed to surrender the person of Suffolk, on the understanding that his life would be spared. Spared it was, but only within the limits of the Tower, until at last Henry VIII brought his own version of reason of state to bear upon him in 1513. For by then, Suffolk's younger brother Richard, after many adventures, which were not to end until his death fighting for Francis I at the battle of Pavia in 1525, had got himself recognized as king of England by Louis XII of France. The fate of Suffolk's next eldest brother, William, was more unfortunate. He had been put in the Tower by Henry VII in 1501, and there he stayed for thirty-eight years until the Reaper brought his release in 1539.

Henry VII at any rate contrived to keep the lists clear

for his own son and heir, and in due course Henry VIII succeeded in 1509 without doubt and difficulty. The bold pronouncement of statute 1 Henry VII, c.1 was vindicated.[1]

Henry Tudor's upbringing and early education until he attained the age of fourteen, was, as we have seen, almost entirely in the household of a powerful and influential Yorkist magnate who was high in the confidence and counsels of Edward IV until the end for him came in 1469. There can be no question but that he was brought up by the Herberts in the expectation that he would in due time

[1] It remained for Henry VIII to eliminate a number of other descendants of Edward III. George, duke of Clarence's daughter, Margaret, countess of Salisbury, was executed in 1541, after having been attainted in 1539 and lodged in the Tower for two years for allegedly compromising correspondence with her own son Reginald Pole, the future Cardinal, who happily for him was out of reach; her eldest son Henry, Lord Montague, had already been eliminated in 1538. The son of Henry, second duke of Buckingham, Edward the third duke, lost his head in 1521, and his grandson, who had the additional misfortune of being the son of Ursula, a daughter of Margaret, countess of Salisbury, suffered a similar fate for overt treason ten years after Henry VIII had passed away. Edward IV's daughter Catherine married William Courtenay, earl of Devon, and their son, Henry, marquis of Exeter actually became heir presumptive to Henry VIII unless or until an heir apparent arrived, but that did not save his head in 1538. These successive liquidations removed all the male potential rivals who were unlucky enough to trace their descent by the wrong lines from Edward III. But there still remained some pruning to be done within the Tudor-Woodville family itself. Henry VIII's own sister Mary, as soon as she became the widow of Louis XII, married Charles Brandon, duke of Suffolk; their daughter Frances in due course married Henry Grey, third marquis of Dorset, the great-grandson of Queen Elizabeth Woodville by her first marriage. Their daughter was Lady Jane Grey, who had the misfortune to marry Lord Guildford Dudley, a son of John Dudley, duke of Northumberland. The exploitation by the latter of the possibilities of these dangerous descents on the death of Edward VI, brought execution to himself, to Lady Jane Grey and her husband, a pardon but still execution on other grounds to her father Henry Grey. By 1554, the Tudors had little left to fear from rival descendants of Edward III, except from those of Henry VIII's sister Margaret in Scotland. Elizabeth I was obliged to assent to the execution of Margaret's grand-daughter Mary, Queen of Scots in 1587, but by 1603 the way was clear for Mary's son James VI to add the inheritance of Tudor to that of Stuart. The headsman's axe had indeed fallen sharply and often before this union of crowns came about; probably needlessly often, but it may well be that in the process the bloodshed of countless innocent could-be and would-be dupes was saved. But it is obvious that Tudor reason of state demanded and obtained far more numerous blood-sacrifices than the Yorkist version did.

come to be an ornament to the Yorkist régime, and that the only knowledge of governmental matters which he was likely to imbibe at that time was derived from the ruling circle of which Herbert was a prominent and ambitious member. After his departure in 1471 to the Continent, Henry's environment changed radically. For intimate company he depended upon those who joined him in exile, of whom at first there were few, and those Lancastrian in origins, including above all his uncle Jasper (who incidentally was at one time well acquainted with Sir John Fortescue, and could scarcely have been ignorant of the latter's ideas on the weaknesses of the old régime). Only latterly did Yorkist malcontents have occasion to share his exile, but these eventually included two important Woodvilles, the marquis of Dorset (for what he was worth), and Sir Edward Woodville. After the *débâcle* of Buckingham's rebellion in 1483, others followed suit, including two able agents of his mother's, Reginald Bray and Christopher Urswick; the former of whom was to remain all his life one of Henry's most trusted and reliable men of business; the latter was to be used in many delicate negotiations, and both were to be among his confidential counsellors. Morton was not far away, and later as Archbishop and Chancellor was to aid him with his wise and experienced counsel all the rest of his life. Otherwise Henry in exile could learn but little about governmental affairs except from what he could see and hear of the ducal court of Brittany, and, during the last year or so, of the court of France. That he learnt much from these sources we can take for granted, for his régime as king showed some distinctly Continental characteristics. These years of exile made an odd but fruitful period of learning, without responsibility or practical experience of government or management, until at length he became king — a long period of reflection and meditation such as none of his predecessors as kings of England had ever had. There can

be no doubt at all that he was a young man of extremely
acute intelligence, who was given by the fates plenty of
years in which to contemplate the problems which might
confront him should he ever become king of England. His
sheer intelligence, not his hereditary descent, was the real
trump-card in the possession of his somewhat forlorn
'party', and upon it the Tudor régime was to be founded.
But it is not surprising that the basic principles of his
government turned out to be markedly Yorkist in character and conception, and that his most enduring achievements were essentially a continuation of the work of the
preceding quarter of a century. Without the rehabilitation
of the kingship and the administrative and financial
reformation which Edward IV had inaugurated and
Richard III had striven to maintain, Henry VII's régime
could scarcely have achieved anything like the success
which it did, within the time it did. There was singularly
little innovation in substance in the government of Henry
VII; almost everything he accomplished in government
and administration followed precedent, Yorkist or earlier.
What was unprecedented was the king's own single-minded
addiction to statecraft, his unshakeable determination to
succeed in his policies, his unerring choice of the right men
for the right jobs, and above all, his powers of perception
combined with firmness of will, such as had not been seen
in a king of England since the days of Edward I, or even
perhaps Henry II, if indeed at any time. Primarily because
of these personal qualities, he was able to realize in practice
far better than the Yorkists the aims of 'politique reule and
governance'. Henry VII's conception of his council and
counsellors did not differ materially from Edward IV's
from 1471. His council was similar in composition to that
of the Yorkists, and a number of his councillors had served
Edward IV or Richard III, or both. He was not encum-
bered with anybody resembling the Nevilles, nor indeed
with any of the older type of magnate opponents. He owed

most to the very people who had joined and counselled him in exile; these were the men who stayed in his counsels permanently, who between them did much to make his régime work, and all of whom remained high in his service for life. He knew how to use his councillors to the best advantage, how to group them for this or that purpose, how to send one councillor here or there according to prevailing needs, how to keep some always near him, how to use 'councillors learned in the law' to see that the law really gave him what was lawfully the king's; how to make use more fully of the judicial discretion always inherent in the king's council, whether sitting in Star Chamber or elsewhere, in the interests of law and order — and, of course, of the king; how to develop further Richard III's idea that some of the councillors might give ear to 'poor men's requests'; how, in short, to make his council supple and alert, responsive and efficient to meet the multifarious needs of the moment, whilst remaining the pliable instrument of his own will and leaving him untrammelled in the exercise of the powers which belonged to the king alone.

Henry's attitude towards parliaments differed in no important way from that of his Yorkist predecessors. He, like them, saw to it (as old Sir John Fortescue had recommended years before, whether Henry knew that or not) that his own financial resources grew great so that he did not have to depend very much upon parliamentary grants, but he was willing enough, as Edward IV had been, to make the most of grants made for warlike purposes, however pacific his own real intentions remained. Only seven parliaments were summoned during the twenty-four years of his reign; of these no fewer than six met in the first half of it, and only one (in 1504) met in the last twelve years — a striking tribute, if not to Henry VII's parliamentary sense, certainly to the overwhelming success of his financial policies. But, nonetheless, even in the few parliaments of his reign, Henry showed that he knew how to turn to the advantage of his government the precedent set in Richard III's one and only parliament — how to dominate proceedings by introducing numerous 'official' bills and enacting them as statutes. It was not that bills introduced by the Commons ceased to appear, but that bills inspired by the government outweighed them in numbers and importance. What in this respect had been something of an innovation under Richard III became under Henry VII more like an established custom. Henry evidently saw the advantage of legislating in this way, and the statute roll became alive with a host of measures designed to re-inforce previous enactments, to correct abuses, to remedy general grievances, to amend the law, to authorize procedures, to promote or in some degree to control economic interests. He showed himself in striking degree a legislator by parliamentary statute, and the example was not lost on his successor Henry VIII nor his mentor, Thomas Cromwell.

But, although a goodly spate of enactments resulted from the parliament of 1504, most of what Henry VII wanted to do in this sphere was complete by 1497, and his financial independence by then enabled him to forgo the issuing of parliamentary summonses for the rest of his reign, except for the occasion of 1504. It was indeed in the financial sphere that Henry VII attained a degree of success which far surpassed that reached by any of his predecessors, partly by profiting from, and carrying much further, the methods of his Yorkist predecessors.

Henry VII was determined upon the 'better endowment of the Crown', and his determination in this matter, we may be sure, was sharpened, not only by his appreciation of the need to avoid the financial weakness which had beset Lancaster and brought the monarchy to bankruptcy, but also by his own personal experiences as a poverty-stricken refugee for at least half of his life-time before he became king. Penury in ambitious youth is often the parent of 'avarice' in later life.

Henry was in a strong position to achieve his aim. He
could not only take over the large territorial possessions of
the Crown as the Yorkists had left them, but could also
add to them those of the earldom of Richmond (the
lawyers got over the difficulty of his attainder by Richard
III with the doctrine that attainder was automatically
erased by his assumption of the Crown), plus the forfeitures
of those who had fought on the losing side at Bosworth,
and later at Stoke, plus again the windfalls coming to him
in consequence of the condemnations for treason which
were to occur during his reign. He could also follow the
example of Edward IV and procure acts of resumption,
even more stringent in scope, which brought back to the
Crown lands previously alienated. Naturally he had to
to make exemptions or fresh alienations of his own in order
to reward or ensure fidelity and service to himself, but he
did so only with discretion and moderation. He could
contrive to extend further the Yorkist devices of securing
the management and collection of revenues from these
vast estates, not by the Exchequer but by specific receivers,
and the payment of the proceeds direct into the Chamber,
which rapidly became, even more prominently than under
the Yorkists, the effective treasury for ready cash, very
close to the king himself, and where he could spend many
an agreeable hour scrutinizing and initialling accounts.
Very likely he took notice of the memorandum on improved financial adminstration which had been prepared
under Richard III's auspices. He could in due course
overhaul the Exchequer machinery itself. He could use in
a variety of financial offices his trusty and able fellow-
exiles, Reginald Bray, Thomas Lovell, and John Heron,
and was sensible enough to continue in lesser offices some
of those who had served the Yorkists.

He saw no reason why the Crown should be cheated out
of revenues which lawfully belonged to it, and risked (and
obtained) much unpopularity and disrepute by the

extreme thoroughness with which he, his 'council learned in the law', his officers and agents evolved and manipulated machinery to squeeze those whom to-day we should probably call simply 'tax-dodgers'. The king could hardly 'live of his own' if he did not in fact get his own, but the process of getting his own inevitably exposed him to accusations of 'avarice' and 'rapacity', especially in matters where traditional sloth, inefficiency, and corruption had commonly prevailed. Henry had become a king who meant business and no nonsense about it. If there were penal statutes the enforcement of which would bring in revenue, then those statutes were to be enforced; if people held land from him technically as feudal tenants-in-chief, then they owed him money on various occasions and would not be allowed to conceal the facts, and the more tenants-in-chief there were, however small, the better. If there were possibilities — and indeed there were many — of increasing revenue from the lawful but strict administration of justice, then by all means let justice be done, even if the bounds of reasonable moderation might sometimes be overstepped. If emergency demanded more ready cash, then let Edward IV's device of getting 'benevolences' be resorted to, despite Richard III's statute to the contrary, for the next parliament could be relied upon to whitewash the transaction.

Nor, when all the proceeds of these and other sources of income were gathered in, would the revenue be frittered away. Expenditure would be controlled carefully, so that the time would come when annual revenue would greatly exceed expenditure, and at long last the king would be enabled to accumulate a very large capital sum. Its accumulation on such a scale was unique in the annals of the kingship, even if Edward IV had managed to accumulate a surplus. It was a pity that a contemporary reporter should have been led by such a phenomenon to have thought fit to describe Henry, when the news of his death

reached him, as a 'very great miser', even if in the next
sentence he admitted that the late king had been 'a very
great man'. But Henry's son and heir (described by the
same writer as 'liberal and handsome') was soon to find
how to dissipate the near two million pounds which his
father had left him.

Henry's demands on his parliaments were not great.
There were precedents for the grant of customs-duties to
a sovereign for life dating back from Richard II's time, but
Henry VII was the first king to receive such a grant in his
first parliament. It is not surprising, with the manifold
efforts of Henry throughout his reign to encourage the
expansion of trade and commerce (even though sometimes
interrupted for political reasons) by all the means in his
power, by statutory provisions, by diplomatic agreements,
by personal interest and example, that the proceeds of the
customs-duties should increase as the reign passed. No
profitable precedents set by Edward IV were lost upon
him. Five of his seven parliaments made grants of some
kind, to meet various 'extra-ordinary' expenses envisaged
at the time. But Henry's 'war-expenses', apart from dealing
with plots at home, turned out to be markedly similiar to
those of Edward IV.

Henry could tackle and solve the problem of the Crown's
poverty, and could tackle, but less completely solve, the
perennial problem of lawlessness and disorder. He could
re-furbish the instruments which already existed for his
purpose, improve upon them, and make them operate
more effectively, but he did not invent much that was new
in this important sphere. After all, he had been a rebel
himself and had won his way to the crown by the sword.
His turbulent subjects did not readily change their habits
of violence and chicane just because Henry Tudor had
become their sovereign lord king. Generations, even
centuries, were to pass before the English acquired a
reputation as law-abiding citizens.

The basic difficulty was to devise effective means of combating the abuse of the common law procedures; it was not a question of the lack of laws against the practices that lay at the root of the trouble. Where the common law had proved inadequate in that respect, statute law had frequently been enacted to supplement it. Henry himself re-enacted, extended, or originated numerous statutes designed to restrict or prohibit such practices as livery and maintenance, retaining by indenture or oath, embracery, corruption of juries, and the like. It was easy enough to make laws on these matters — Henry's predecessors had done so often — but far more difficult to enforce them. It was part and parcel of the re-invigorated monarchy of Henry VII that he was able to enforce such laws a good deal better than his predecessors. For one thing there were now few if any over-mighty subjects left who could hope to defy the new king and his council for long. There was nothing new in the Council's adjudicating upon such matters as these (and others), whether in Star Chamber or elsewhere, but it would probably be fair to say that the use made in Henry VII's time of such conciliar jurisdiction went far to confirm the development of the court of Star Chamber which was to be such a formidable feature of the later Tudor régime. We now know that the statutory attempt of 1487 (the so-called Star Chamber Act) to set up a special tribunal to deal with such offences, not only had nothing to do with Star Chamber, but also in fact was a failure, because the tribunal which it did establish proved to be superfluous. The work it was intended to do was already being done and continued to be done by the Council in Star Chamber, and it continued to need to be done long after Henry VII's time.

Another respect in which Henry VII was able to utilize pre-existing instruments and to point the way to future developments was in his handling of local government. He realized the essential need for more effective agents of justice and administration in the localities. Part of the reason for the difficulty in enforcing the law had for long been the decline of the sheriffs as effective officers of the Crown in the shires. This process of decline had been apparent from the fourteenth century, and even then had been partially met by the development of the powers, especially the judicial powers, of the justices of the peace. The decline of the sheriffs, the rise of the justices of the peace, and the inter-related developments in the powers of the various travelling justices which the king's court had been sending out on circuits for generations, were all complex processes. But it is probably reasonable to suppose that Henry VII appreciated the potentiality of the justices of the peace as local agents, judicial and administrative; certainly he still further developed their powers, and was able to keep sufficient control over them, so that they were destined to become the characteristic local instruments of the central government, and to give to Tudor England its most conspicuous feature in that sphere.

In all these, and other ways, Henry VII succeeded in stabilizing a monarchy which was novel in the sense that it brought unwonted efficiency into its undertakings, novel in its unheard-of solvency, and novel in its calm, methodical, unremitting determination to make its government work in practice as no government had worked before. It was novel also in the sense that the new king proved to be a professional king who devoted his whole mind and energy to his profession.

The same dispassionate, calculating mentality which Henry VII brought to bear upon affairs at home, he turned towards foreign affairs as well. It has been said, with considerable justice, that 'the foreign policy of Henry VII was really the mainspring of his government'. For not only did the prestige and the commercial prosperity of the realm depend upon it, but the maintenance of himself and his dynasty upon the throne was bound up with it. Unlike

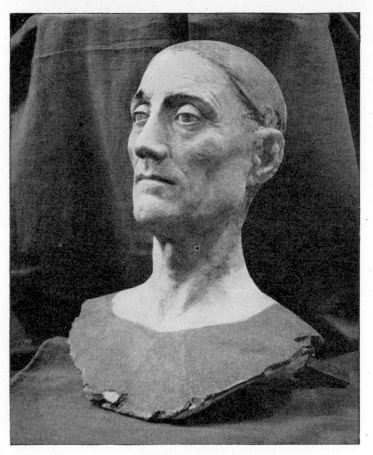

Henry VII

Death mask in Westminster Abbey

any of his predecessors, since at any rate the Angevins, he himself had plenty of opportunity before he came to the throne of observing and experiencing only too intimately the consequences of the support or hostility of European rulers. Undoubtedly he learnt his diplomacy in a hard school, and emerged from it a master of the art and craft. From a mere successful adventurer, a *protégé* of the court of France, who threw all he had on the gamble of August 1485, he diplomatized his way into a position in which sooner or later his hostility was feared and his friendship sought at one time or another by all the principal rulers of Europe. He compelled them to recognize him; he frustrated all their attempts to make use of impostors, pretenders, and cat's-paws against him. He could bluster and threaten France in much the same way as Edward IV had done before him, and in the Treaty of Étâples of 1492 he could substantially re-impose Edward IV's Treaty of Picquigny, and similarly extract financial tribute from the king of France. He could at length procure the marriage of his eldest son, Arthur, to one of the daughters of Spain, and so arrange matters (even if with much hesitation and delay, not to mention shabby dealings) that, for better or for worse, his eventually only surviving son and his own successor should marry Arthur's widow; he could solve the problem of Scotland by marrying one of his daughters to King James IV, and betroth the other daughter to the heir of all the Spanish and Hapsburg domains, even if in fact she married Louis XII of France.

His successes were astonishing, but by no means unrelieved by failures. He could not prevent the acquisition of Brittany by the crown of France; he could not interfere effectively in French and Spanish expansion in Italy; he could not do much to extend the scope of English influence in Ireland, even though he could tighten up the government of the Pale; he could not (after his queen had died in 1503) clinch any of his own matrimonial projects (some of them far more preposterous than Richard III's alleged designs on his niece), including plans for marrying his own daughter-in-law Katherine after Arthur's death, the mad Joanna of Castile (mad or not she could still bear children), Margaret of Savoy, and Joanna of Naples (the charms of whose person he required his envoys to report upon in extreme detail). All these projects, and indeed the diplomacy of which they formed a part, came to nothing, and the foreign policies of his last years were mostly a failure.

But, all in all, Henry VII could well be satisfied with his life's work. He had achieved more than he could have imagined possible in the precarious days of 1485. By 1509 he had assured for England possibilities of future greatness and expansion far beyond the limits of his own prediction; for himself he had secured immortal fame as one of the greatest practitioners of statecraft who has ever worn the crown of England's sovereign.

Conclusion

No serious historian today would subscribe to the old-fashioned idea that the year 1485 in itself marked any particular turning-point in English history. Nonetheless the battle of Bosworth field undoubtedly, as it turned out, did mark an important turning-point in dynastic history. No one, at the time, of course, could possibly have known that for certain. They knew that Richard III and his principal supporters had come to the end of their careers, and that the main Yorkist line could have slight chance of a restoration. They very soon recognized the fact that Henry Tudor had assumed the Crown, but they could not know that the last major battle in the dynastic civil wars had been fought. They could not tell for how long, and to what effect, the new king would be able to hold on to what he had gained. Henry was a figure totally unknown to almost all of his suddenly acquired subjects. Few lamented Richard III, but many had reason to regret the termination of twenty-five years of Yorkist reign; quite a lot of them had never known any other rule. The mass of them no doubt were glad to persuade themselves that the period of civil war had ended, but then many would have supposed that that had already occurred at Tewkesbury in 1471, and some at least of these would have regarded Henry's incursion and the battle of Bosworth as a re-opening of the whole issue. Inevitably it took time for people to appreciate that Bosworth was not the beginning of fresh disturbance, but virtually the end of it. They could realize that better and with more confidence after the battle of Stoke in 1487, and the death there of Richard III's recognized heir presumptive.

There are some historians who think that dynastic history is of small account, and that the civil wars of the fifteenth century, so erroneously and misleadingly called the 'Wars of the Roses' were no more than the fights of kites and crows. But they are wrong. The civil wars of that century were not about roses, badges, or other symbols, nor were they mere faction fights nor lawless squabbles among baronial brigands. They were about the most vital political problem which confronted men at that time and for centuries thereafter, namely, in whom and therefore in what family were the all-important powers of the kingship to be vested? Government is always a vital matter, upon which the life of the people and realm depends; in those days, and for centuries thereafter, the king *was* the government. For a thousand years or so before, the kings had governed, according to their lights, and the whole history of England was bound up with the question of how the kings had governed. Government depended upon the personal character, ability, and initiative of the king himself, his choice of ministers, and his policies.

It was unfortunate that the events of 1399 had completely upset the traditional method of settling the question of who was to be king. The usurpation of Henry IV hopelessly undermined the habitual solution to the problem of the succession to the Crown. The displacement of the lawful king and the multiplication of Edward III's descendants made a firm solution difficult. The problem might indeed have been evaded if Henry IV's own direct heirs had succeeded in governing to the general satisfaction, but they did not. In all the prevalent circumstances, there was no hope that the answer to the fundamental problem could be found without resort to the arguments of force. For no one answer was possible which was acceptable to all the numerous and powerful interests concerned. It was not to be expected that one interest could readily impose a solution upon all the others, until such time as those others

N

had dwindled in number and resources and could be induced to submit. For the issue was grave and fundamental, and the earthly prize at stake was the greatest to which any Englishman could aspire.

It seemed, from 1471 at least, that Edward IV had found the solution, and undoubtedly he succeeded in arresting the decline of the kingship, in reviving and improving markedly the working of government, and in the process he did much to set the realm on the paths which it was to follow thereafter indefinitely. Richard III sought to ensure that those paths would continue to be trodden, but he could not do it without aberrations of his own too great to be generally acceptable.

It is tolerably certain that if Henry Tudor had happened to be a man of lesser calibre than he was (as he might so easily have been), then Bosworth and Stoke would not in fact have been the end of the civil wars, and stability of government might have remained only a dream incapable of fulfilment for another generation.

But as it turned out, Henry was the very man for the job. He took over the Yorkist monarchy, used its methods and institutions, extended them, improved them, instilled into them the spirit and energy of a new efficiency. He thereby ensured that the realm of England should not lack a vigorous, and in the then sense of the term a 'modern government'. The old monarchy took on a new look, but at the same time remained not simply the Tudor Monarchy, nor the Yorkist Monarchy. It was also still the monarchy of Lancaster, of Plantagenet, of the Angevins, of the Normans and of the Anglo-Saxons. It was at once New and Old, and because it was both old and new, it endured.

Books for Further Reading

FEW satisfactory books covering the whole period are extant. Sir James Ramsay, *Lancaster and York* (2 vols. 1892), is a valuable source of information, largely in the form of annals, with a minimum of interpretation, and although of little use except for the sequence of political events, is nonetheless indispensable. The third volume of William Stubbs's *Constitutional History of England* (which volume was first published in 1878) contains an invaluable survey of fifteenth-century English history, political as well as constitutional, but is out of date on most matters of interpretation. The volume by Sir Charles Oman on the period 1377–1485 in the *Political History of England* and *England in the later Middle Ages* by K. H. Vickers (1913) have been largely superseded by later work. A more up-to-date and useful survey of the whole period is to be found in A. R. Myers's *England in the Late Middle Ages* (Pelican Books, 1952). The *Oxford History of England* has two volumes relevant to the period; the first of these, on the fourteenth century, is by May McKisack (1959). The second of them, on the fifteenth century, is by E. F. Jacob (1961). Volumes VII and VIII of the *Cambridge Medieval History* contain a number of valuable chapters on both English and European topics within the period. Both these volumes and the two volumes in the *Oxford History* provide very full bibliographies, exhaustive of printed material up to the dates of publication.

Among more specialized studies may be mentioned: E. Perroy, *The Hundred Years' War*, (English edition 1952); A. Steel, *Richard II* (1941) and *The Receipt of the Exchequer, 1377–1485* (1954); S. B. Chrimes *English Constitutional Ideas in the Fifteenth Century* (1936); R. W. Somerville, *History of the Duchy of Lancaster*, (vol. I of which was published in 1953), is indispensable for an understanding of the complicated history of the Duchy; C. L. Kingford's essays, published under the title *Prejudice and Promise in the Fifteenth Century* (1925) has some still valuable contributions; H. T. Evans, *Wales and the Wars of the Roses* (1915) has interesting information; Margaret Hastings, *The Court of Common Pleas in the Fifteenth Century*, a very readable book on a technical subject. H. L. Gray, *The Influence of the Commons on Early Legislation* (1932), contains some useful material; J. S. Roskell, *The Commons in the Parliament of 1422* (1954) is valuable. Some of the writings of Sir John Fortescue may be consulted in the *Governance of England*, ed. by C. Plummer (1885) and *De Laudibus Legum Anglie*, ed. and trans. by S. B. Chrimes (1942, repr. 1949). *Select Documents of English Constitutional History, 1307–1485*, ed. by S. B. Chrimes and A. L. Brown (1961) provides texts illustrative of constitutional developments within the period. J. G. Dickinson, *The Congress of Arras, 1435* (1955) is an interesting study of medieval diplomacy.

The Yorkist period is still by far the most neglected period in English history. Few general books on that period can be recommended with confidence. Much detailed research will be needed before our state of knowledge of it can become comparable with our knowledge of the preceding and succeeding periods. Some valuable work has been done in recent years and is to be found in the articles referred to below. The most detailed study of the reign of Edward IV is that by Cora L. Scofield (2 vols. 1923) under the title of *The Life and Reign of Edward IV*, a mine of information, much of it from unprinted sources, but a mine which needs laborious quarrying to yield its gold. A more amateurish but more readable short account of *Edward IV* is that by L. Stratford (1910). A useful, even if now somewhat old-fashioned study of *Warwick the King-Maker*, is that by Sir Charles Oman (1893). A more recent study of Warwick under the title of *The King-Maker*, is that by P. M. Kendall (1957), which is readable, even if it lacks perspective and tends to exaggerate in some respects the importance of its subject. P. M. Kendall has also provided a fresh study of *Richard III* (1955) which endeavours to reconsider the reign of Richard III in the light of modern research, but is based in part upon an imaginative reconstruction of some of the more mysterious episodes in that controversial period. It has the advantage, however, of not accepting, without close criticism, Sir Thomas

More's version, and in that respect improves upon the standard life of *Richard III* by J. Gairdner (rev. ed. 1898), which has otherwise not been superseded for the purposes of scholarship, and which, incidentally, contains in an appendix the fullest account extant of the adventures of Perkin Warbeck. C. A. J. Armstrong's discovery of a contemporary chronicle by Dominic Mancini, and his publication of it with translation and notes under the title of *De Occupatione Regni Anglie per Riccardum tercium* (1936), added considerably to the materials for the reign of Richard III. W. H. Dunham, *Lord Hastings' 'Indentured Retainers', 1461–1485* (1955) is a valuable study. P. M. Kendall's recent *The Yorkist Age* (1962) gives lively pictures in the sphere of social history.

Among recent articles of major importance for the period are: C. A. J. Armstrong, 'The Inauguration Ceremonies of the Yorkist Kings and their Titles to the Throne', in *Transactions of the Royal Historical Society*, 4th ser., XXX (1948); A. Steel, 'The Financial Background of the Wars of the Roses' in *History*, new ser., XL (1955); B. P. Wolffe, 'The Management of English Royal Estates under the Yorkist Kings' in *English Historical Review*, LXXI (1956); G. L. Harriss, 'The Struggle for Calais: An Aspect of the Rivalry between Lancaster and York' in ibid., LXXV (1960); J. R. Lander, 'The Yorkist Council and Administration' in ibid., LXXIII (1958); 'Edward IV: The Modern Legend and a Revision' in *History*, new ser., XLI (1956); and also 'Council, Administration, and Councillors, 1461 to 1485', in *Bulletin of the Institute of Historical Research*, XXXII (1959); 'Attainder and Forfeiture, 1453 to 1509' in *The Historical Journal*, IV (1961). R. J. Knecht; 'The Episcopate and the Wars of the Roses' in *University of Birmingham Historical Journal*, VI (1958); Mortimer Levine, 'Richard III — Usurper or Lawful King?' in *Speculum*, *34* (1959). A useful summary of arguments is contained in Appendix V, 'The Princes in the Tower', *The Complete Peerage*, vol. XII, pt. 2 (1959).

Much the most detailed study of the reign of Henry VII is that by Wilhelm Busch, *England under the Tudors*, vol. I, *Henry VII*, (English edition, 1895), and this is still the most comprehensive book on the reign, although it is much out of date on the institutional and financial aspects. The reign has received more succint and more up-to-date treatment by J. D. Mackie in the *Oxford History of England* volume on *The Early Tudors* (1952), and by G. R. Elton in *England under the Tudors* (1955). Governmental aspects of the reign were examined by K. M. P. Pickthorn in the first volume of his *Early Tudor Government* (1934). Convenient source material may be found in A. F. Pollard, *The Reign of Henry VII from Contemporary Sources* (3 vols., 1913–14) and in J. R. Tanner, *Tudor Constitutional Documents* (2nd ed. 1930), now superseded by G. R. Elton, *The Tudor Constitution: Documents and Commentary* (1960). *Select Cases in the Council of Henry VII*, ed. C. G. Bayne (Selden Society, vol. 75, 1958), contains a valuable introduction to its subject. G. R. Elton's article 'Henry VII: Rapacity and Remorse' in *The Historical Journal*, I (1958), suggests some correctives of commonly accepted views, but it should be read with J. P. Cooper, 'Henry VII's last years Reconsidered', in ibid., II (1959), and G. R. Elton's riposte *'Henry VII: A Restatement'* in ibid., IV (1961).

A useful survey of the available literature is contained in Margaret Hastings 'High History or Hack History: England in the Later Middle Ages' in *Speculum*, XXXVI (1961).

Index

PRINTED IN GREAT BRITAIN BY ROBERT MACLEHOSE AND CO. LTD
THE UNIVERSITY PRESS, GLASGOW